Agnes Repplier

Essays in Idleness

Agnes Repplier

Essays in Idleness

ISBN/EAN: 9783744651875

Printed in Europe, USA, Canada, Australia, Japan

Cover: Foto ©Thomas Meinert / pixelio.de

More available books at **www.hansebooks.com**

ESSAYS IN IDLENESS

BY

AGNES REPPLIER

BOSTON AND NEW YORK
HOUGHTON, MIFFLIN AND COMPANY
The Riverside Press, Cambridge
1895

To AGNES IRWIN.

CONTENTS.

"Leisure" is reprinted from "Scribner's Magazine" by permission of the publishers.

ESSAYS IN IDLENESS.

AGRIPPINA.

SHE is sitting now on my desk, and I glance at her with deference, mutely begging permission to begin. But her back is turned to me, and expresses in every curve such fine and delicate disdain that I falter and lose courage at the very threshold of my task. I have long known that cats are the most contemptuous of creatures, and that Agrippina is the most contemptuous of cats. The spirit of Bouhaki, the proud Theban beast that sat erect, with gold earrings in his ears, at the feet of his master, King Hana ; the spirit of Muezza, whose slumbers Mahomet himself was not bold enough to disturb ; the spirit of Micetto, Chateaubriand's ecclesiastical pet, dignified as a cardinal, and conscious ever that he was the gift of a sovereign pontiff, — the spirits of all

arrogant cats that have played scornful parts in
the world's great comedy look out from Agrippina's yellow eyes, and hold me in subjection.
I should like to explain to her, if I dared,
that my desk is small, littered with many
papers, and sadly overcrowded with the useful
inutilities which affectionate friends delight in
giving me at Christmas time. Sainte-Beuve's
cat, I am aware, sat on his desk, and roamed
at will among those precious manuscripts
which no intrusive hand was ever permitted to
touch ; but Sainte-Beuve probably had sufficient space reserved for his own comfort and
convenience. I have not; and Agrippina's
beautifully ringed tail flapping across my copy
distracts my attention, and imperils the neat-
ness of my penmanship. Even when she is
disposed to be affable, turns the light of her
countenance upon me, watches with attentive
curiosity every stroke I make, and softly, with
curved paw, pats my pen as it travels over the
paper, — even in these halcyon moments,
though my self-love is flattered by her condescension, I am aware that I should work better and more rapidly if I denied myself this
charming companionship.

But in truth it is impossible for a lover of cats to banish these alert, gentle, and discriminating little friends, who give us just enough of their regard and complaisance to make us hunger for more. M. Fée, the naturalist, who has written so admirably about animals, and who understands, as only a Frenchman can understand, the delicate and subtle organization of a cat, frankly admits that the keynote of its character is independence. It dwells under our roof, sleeps by our fire, endures our blandishments, and apparently enjoys our society, without for one moment forfeiting its sense of absolute freedom, without acknowledging any servile relation to the human creature who shelters it. "The cat," says M. Fée, "will never part with its liberty; it will neither be our servant, like the horse, nor our friend, like the dog. It consents to live as our guest; it accepts the home we offer and the food we give; it even goes so far as to solicit our caresses, but capriciously, and when it suits its humor to receive them."

Rude and masterful souls resent this fine self-sufficiency in a domestic animal, and require that it should have no will but theirs,

no pleasure that does not emanate from them.
They are forever prating of the love and fidelity of the dog, of the beast that obeys their
slightest word, crouches contentedly for hours
at their feet, is exuberantly grateful for the
smallest attention, and so affectionate that its
demonstrations require to be curbed rather
than encouraged.   All this homage is pleasing
to their vanity; yet there are people, less ma-
gisterial perhaps, or less exacting, who believe
that true friendship, even with an animal, may
be built upon mutual esteem and independence ;
that to demand gratitude is to be unworthy of
it ; and that obedience is not essential to agreeable and healthy intercourse.   A man who
owns a dog is, in every sense of the word, its
master ; the term expresses accurately their
mutual relations.   But it is ridiculous when
applied to the limited possession of a cat.   I
am certainly not Agrippina's mistress, and the
assumption of authority on my part would be
a mere empty dignity, like those swelling titles
which afford such innocent delight to the
Freemasons of our severe republic.   If I call
Agrippina, she does not come ; if I tell her to
go away, she remains where she is; if I try to

persuade her to show off her one or two little accomplishments, she refuses, with courteous but unswerving decision. She has frolicsome moods, in which a thimble, a shoe-buttoner, a scrap of paper, or a piece of string will drive her wild with delight; she has moods of inflexible gravity, in which she stares solemnly at her favorite ball rolling over the carpet, without stirring one lazy limb to reach it. "Have I seen this foolish toy before?" she seems to be asking herself with musing austerity; "and can it be possible that there are cats who run after such frivolous trifles? Vanity of vanities, and all is vanity, save only to lie upon the hearth-rug, and be warm, and 'think grave thoughts to feed a serious soul.'" In such moments of rejection and humiliation, I comfort myself by recalling the words of one too wise for arrogance. "When I play with my cat," says Montaigne, "how do I know whether she does not make a jest of me? We entertain each other with mutual antics; and if I have my own time for beginning or refusing, she too has hers."

This is the spirit in which we should approach a creature so reserved and so utterly

self-sufficing ; this is the only key we have to
that natural distinction of character which re-
pels careless and unobservant natures.   When
I am told that Agrippina is disobedient, ungrateful, cold-hearted, perverse, stupid, treacherous, and cruel, I no longer strive to check
the torrent of abuse.   I know that Buffon said
all this, and much more, about cats, and that
people have gone on repeating it ever since,
principally because these spirited little beasts
have remained just what it pleased Providence
to make them, have preserved their primitive
freedom through centuries of effete and demor-
alizing civilization.   Why, I wonder, should a
great many good men and women cherish an
unreasonable grudge against one animal because it does not chance to possess the precise
qualities of another?   " My dog fetches my
slippers for me every night," said a friend
triumphantly, not long ago.   " He puts them
first to warm by the fire, and then brings them
over to my chair, wagging his tail, and as
proud as Punch.   Would your cat do as much
for you, I 'd like to know ? "   Assuredly not !
If I waited for Agrippina to fetch me shoes or
slippers, I should have no other resource save

to join as speedily as possible one of the bare-
footed religious orders of Italy. But, after all,
fetching slippers is not the whole duty of domestic pets. As La Fontaine gently reminds
us : —

" Tout animal n'a pas toutes propriétés."

We pick no quarrel with a canary because it
does not talk like a parrot, nor with a parrot
because it does not sing like a canary. We
find no fault with a King Charles spaniel for
not flying at the throat of a burglar, nor with
a St. Bernard because we cannot put it in our
pocket. Agrippina will never make herself
serviceable, yet nevertheless is she of inestima-
ble service. How many times have I rested
tired eyes on her graceful little body, curled
up in a ball and wrapped round with her tail
like a parcel ; or stretched out luxuriously on
my bed, one paw coyly covering her face, the
other curved gently inwards, as though clasp-
ing an invisible treasure ! Asleep or awake,
in rest or in motion, grave or gay, Agrippina
is always beautiful ; and it is better to be
beautiful than to fetch and carry from the
rising to the setting of the sun. She is droll,
too, with an unconscious humor, even in her

most serious and sentimental moods. She has
quite the longest ears that ever were seen on so
small a cat, eyes more solemn than Athene's
owl blinking in the sunlight, and an air of
supercilious disdain that would have made
Diogenes seem young and ardent by her side.
Sitting on the library table, under the evening
lamp, with her head held high in air, her tall
ears as erect as chimneys, and her inscrutable
gaze fixed on the darkest corner of the room,
Agrippina inspires in the family sentiments of
mingled mirthfulness and awe. To laugh at
her in such moments, however, is to incur her
supreme displeasure. I have known her to
jump down from the table, and walk haugh-
tily out of the room, because of a single half-
suppressed but wholly indecorous giggle.

Schopenhauer has said that the reason domestic pets are so lovable and so helpful to
us is because they enjoy, quietly and placidly,
the present moment. Life holds no future for
them, and consequently no care ; if they are
content, their contentment is absolute ; and
our jaded and wearied spirits find a natural
relief in the sight of creatures whose little cups
of happiness can so easily be filled to the brim.

Walt Whitman expresses the same thought more coarsely when he acknowledges that he loves the society of animals because they do not sweat and whine over their condition, nor lie awake in the dark and weep for their sins, nor sicken him with discussions of their duty. In truth, that admirable counsel of Sydney Smith's, "Take short views of life," can be obeyed only by the brutes; for the thought that travels even to the morrow is long enough to destroy our peace of mind, inasmuch as we know not what the morrow may bring forth. But when Agrippina has breakfasted, and washed, and sits in the sunlight blinking at me with affectionate contempt, I feel soothed by her absolute and unqualified enjoyment. I know how full my day will be of things that I don't want particularly to do, and that are not particularly worth doing; but for her, time and the world hold only this brief moment of contentment. Slowly the eyes close, gently the little body is relaxed. Oh, you who strive to relieve your overwrought nerves, and cultivate power through repose, watch the exquisite languor of a drowsy cat, and despair of imitating such perfect and restful grace!

There is a gradual yielding of every muscle to
the soft persuasiveness of slumber; the flexible frame is curved into tender lines, the head
nestles lower, the paws are tucked out of sight;
no convulsive throb or start betrays a rebellious alertness; only a faint quiver of unconscious satisfaction, a faint heaving of the tawny
sides, a faint gleam of the half-shut yellow
eyes, and Agrippina is asleep. I look at her
for one wistful moment, and then turn resolutely to my work. It were ignoble to wish
myself in her place, and yet how charming to
be able to settle down to a nap, *sans peur et
sans reproche*, at ten o'clock in the morning!

These, then, are a few of the pleasures to be
derived from the society of an amiable cat;
and by an amiable cat I mean one that, while
maintaining its own dignity and delicate reserve, is nevertheless affable and condescend-
ing in the company of human beings. There
is nothing I dislike more than newspaper and
magazine stories about priggish pussies — like
the children in Sunday-school books — that
share their food with hungry beasts from the
back alleys, and show touching fidelity to old
blind masters, and hunt partridges, in a spirit

of noble self-sacrifice, for consumptive mis-
tresses, and scorn to help themselves to delica-
cies from the kitchen tables, and arouse their
households so often in cases of fire that I
should suspect them of starting the conflagra-
tions in order to win applause by giving the
alarm. Whatever a real cat may or may not
be, it is never a prig, and all true lovers of the
race have been quick to recognize and appreciate this fact.

"I value in the cat," says Chateaubriand,
"that independent and almost ungrateful temper which prevents it from attaching itself to
any one ; the indifference with which it passes
from the salon to the housetop. When you
caress it, it stretches itself out and arches its
back responsively ; but that is caused by physical pleasure, and not, as in the case of the
dog, by a silly satisfaction in loving and being
faithful to a master who returns thanks in
kicks. The cat lives alone, has no need of
society, does not obey except when it likes, pre-
tends to sleep that it may see the more clearly,
and scratches everything that it can scratch."

Here is a sketch spirited enough, and of good
outline, but hardly correct in detail. A cat

seldom manifests affection, yet is often distinctly social, and likes to see itself the petted
minion of a family group. Agrippina, in fact,
so far from living alone, will not, if she can
help it, remain for a moment in a room by herself. She is content to have me as a companion, perhaps in default of better; but if I
go upstairs or downstairs in search of a book,
or my eyeglasses, or any one of the countless
things that are never where they ought to be,
Agrippina follows closely at my heels. Sometimes, when she is fast asleep, I steal softly
out of the door, thinking to escape her vigilance; but before I have taken a dozen steps
she is under my feet, mewing a gentle reproach, and putting on all the injured airs of
a deserted Ariadne. I should like to think
such behavior prompted by affection rather
than by curiosity; but in my candid moments
I find this " pathetic fallacy " a difficult sentiment to cherish. There are people, I am
aware, who trustfully assert that their pets
love them; and one such sanguine creature
has recently assured the world that " no man
who boasts the real intimacy and confidence
of a cat would dream of calling his four-footed

friend 'puss.' " But is not such a boast
rather ill-timed at best? How dare any man
venture to assert that he possesses the intimacy
and confidence of an animal so exclusive and
so reserved? I doubt if Cardinal Wolsey, in
the zenith of his pride and power, claimed the
intimacy and confidence of the superb cat who
sat in a cushioned armchair by his side, and
reflected with mimic dignity the full-blown
honors of the Lord High Chancellor of England. Agrippina, I am humbly aware, grants
me neither her intimacy nor her confidence,
but only her companionship, which I endeavor
to receive modestly, and without flaunting my
favors to the world. She is displeased and
even downcast when I go out, and she greets
my return with delight, thrusting her little
gray head between the banisters the instant
I open the house door, and waving a welcome
in mid-air with one ridiculously small paw.
Being but mortal, I am naturally pleased with
these tokens of esteem, but I do not, on that
account, go about with arrogant brow, and
boast of my intimacy with Agrippina. I
should be laughed at, if I did, by everybody
who is privileged to possess and appreciate a
cat.

As for curiosity, that vice which the Abbé
Galiani held to be unknown to animals, but
which the more astute Voltaire detected in
every little dog that he saw peering out of the
window of its master's coach, it is the ruling
passion of the feline breast. A closet door left
ajar, a box with half-closed lid, an open bureau
drawer, — these are the objects that fill a cat
with the liveliest interest and delight. Agrippina watches breathlessly the unfastening of
a parcel, and tries to hasten matters by clutch-
ing actively at the string. When its contents
are shown her, she examines them gravely,
and then, with a sigh of relief, settles down to
repose. The slightest noise disturbs and irri-
tates her until she discovers its cause. If she
hears a footstep in the hall, she runs out to
see whose it is, and, like certain troublesome
little people I have known, she dearly loves
to go to the front door every time the bell
is rung. From my window she surveys the
street with tranquil scrutiny, and, if boys are
playing below, she follows their games with a
steady, scornful stare, very different from the
wistful eagerness of a friendly dog, quiver-
ing to join in the sport. Sometimes the boys

catch sight of her, and shout up rudely at her window; and I can never sufficiently admire Agrippina's conduct upon these trying occasions, the well-bred composure with which she affects neither to see nor to hear them, nor to be aware that there are such objectionable creatures as children in the world. Sometimes, too, the terrier that lives next door comes out to sun himself in the street, and, beholding my cat sitting well out of reach, he dances madly up and down the pavement, barking with all his might, and rearing himself on his short hind legs, in a futile attempt to dislodge her. Then the spirit of evil enters Agrippina's little heart. The window is open, and she creeps to the extreme edge of the stone sill, stretches herself at full length, peers down smilingly at the frenzied dog, dangles one paw enticingly in the air, and exerts herself with quiet malice to drive him to desperation. Her sense of humor is awakened by his frantic efforts, and by her own absolute security; and not until he is spent with exertion, and lies panting and exhausted on the bricks, does she arch her graceful back, stretch her limbs lazily in the sun, and with one light bound spring from the window to my desk. Wisely has Moncrif observed that a cat is not merely diverted by everything that moves, but is convinced that all nature is occupied exclusively with catering to her diversion.

There is a charming story told by M. Champfleury, who has written so much and so admirably about cats, of a poor hermit whose piety and asceticism were so great that in a vision he was permitted to behold his place in heaven, next to that of St. Gregory, the sovereign pontiff of Christendom. The hermit, who possessed nothing upon earth but a female cat, was abashed by the thought that in the next world he was destined to rank with so powerful a prince of the Church ; and perhaps — for who knows the secret springs of spiritual pride ? — he fancied that his self-inflicted poverty would win for him an even higher reward. Whereupon a second revelation made known to him that his detachment from the world was by no means so complete as he imagined, for that he loved and valued his cat, the sole companion of his solitude, more than St. Gregory loved and valued all his earthly possessions. The Pope on his throne was the truer ascetic of the two.

This little tale conveys to us, in addition to its excellent moral, — never more needed than at present, — a pleasing truth concerning the lovability of cats. While they have never attained, and never deserve to attain, the widespread and somewhat commonplace popularity of dogs, their fascination is a more potent and irresistible charm. He who yields himself to the sweet seductiveness of a cat is beguiled forever from the simple, honorable friendship of the more generous and open-hearted beast. The small domestic sphinx whose inscrutable eyes never soften with affection ; the fetich animal that comes down to us from the far past, adored, hated, and feared, — a god in wise and silent Egypt, a plaything in old Rome, a hunted and unholy creature, suffering one long martyrdom throughout the half-seen, dimly-fathomed Middle Ages, — even now this lovely, uncanny pet is capable of inspiring mingled sentiments of horror and devotion. Those who are under its spell rejoice in their thralldom, and, like M. Champfleury's hermit, grow strangely wed-

ded to this mute, unsympathetic comradeship.
Those who have inherited the old, half-fear-
ful aversion render a still finer tribute to the
cat's native witchery and power. I have seen
middle-aged women, of dignified and tranquil
aspect, draw back with unfeigned dismay at
the sight of Agrippina, a little ball of gray
and yellow fur, curled up in peaceful slumber on the hearth rug. And this instinctive
shrinking has nothing in common with the
perfectly reasonable fear we entertain for a
terrier snapping and snarling at our heels,
or for a mastiff the size of a calf, which our
friend assures us is as gentle as a baby, but
which looks able and ready to tear us limb
from limb. It may be ignominious to be
afraid of dogs, but the emotion is one which
will bear analysis and explanation; we know
exactly what it is we fear; while the uneasi-
ness with which many people behold a harmless and perfectly indifferent cat is a faint
reflection of that superstitious terror which
the nineteenth century still borrows occasionally from the ninth. We call it by a different name, and account for it on purely natural
principles, in deference to progress; but the

Mediæval peasant who beheld his cat steal
out, like a gray shadow, on St. John's Eve, to
join in unholy rites, felt the same shuddering
abhorrence which we witness and wonder at
to-day. He simplified matters somewhat, and
eased his troubled mind by killing the beast;
for cats that ventured forth on the feast of
St. John, or on Halloween, or on the second
Wednesday in Lent, did so at their peril.
Fires blazed for them in every village, and
even quiet stay-at-homes were too often hunted
from their chimney-corners to a cruel death.
There is a receipt signed in 1575 by one
Lucas Pommoreux, — abhorred forever be his
name! — to whom has been paid the sum of a
hundred *sols parisis* " for having supplied for
three years all the cats required for the fire on
St. John's Day;" and be it remembered that
the gracious child, afterwards Louis XIII.,
interceded with Henry IV. for the lives of
these poor animals, sacrificed to wicked sport
and an unreasoning terror.

Girt around with fear, and mystery, and subtle associations of evil, the cat comes down to
us through the centuries; and from every land
fresh traditions of sorcery claim it for their

own.   In Brittany is still whispered the dreadful tale of the cats that danced with sacrile-
gious glee around the crucifix until their king
was slain; and in Sicily men know that if
a black cat serves seven masters in turn he
carries the soul of the seventh into hell.   In
Russia black cats become devils at the end of
seven years, and in southern Europe they are
merely serving their apprenticeship as witches.
Norwegian folk-lore is rich in ghastly stories
like that of the wealthy miller whose mill has
been twice burned down on Whitsun night,
and for whom a traveling tailor offers to keep
watch.   The tailor chalks a circle on the floor,
writes the Lord's prayer around it, and waits
until midnight, when a troop of cats rush in,
and hang a great pot of pitch over the fire-
place.   Again and again they try to overturn
this pitch, but every time the tailor frightens
them away ; and when their leader endeavors
stealthily to draw him outside of his magic
circle, he cuts off her paw with his knife.
Then they all fly howling into the night, and
the next morning the miller sees with joy his
mill standing whole and unharmed.   But the
miller's wife cowers under the bedclothes, of-

fering her left hand to the tailor, and hiding as best she can her right arm's bleeding stump.

Finer even than this tale is the well-known story which " Monk " Lewis told to Shelley of a gentleman who, late one night, went to visit a friend living on the outskirts of a forest in east Germany. He lost his path, and, after wandering aimlessly for some time, beheld at last a light streaming from the windows of an old and ruined abbey. Looking in, he saw a procession of cats lowering into the grave a small coffin with a crown upon it. The sight filled him with horror, and, spurring his horse, he rode away as fast as he could, never stopping until he reached his destination, long after midnight. His friend was still awaiting him, and at once he recounted what had happened; whereupon a cat that lay sleeping by the fire sprang to its feet, cried out, " Then I am the King of the Cats ! " and disappeared like a flash up the chimney.

For my part, I consider this the best cat story in all literature, full of suggestiveness and terror, yet picturesque withal, and leaving ample room in the mind for speculation. Why was not the heir apparent bidden to the royal funeral? Was there a disputed succession, and how are such points settled in the mysterious domain of cat-land? The notion that these animals gather in ghost-haunted churches and castles for their nocturnal revels is one common to all parts of Europe. We remember how the little maiden of the "Mountain Idyl" confides to Heine that the innocent-looking cat in the chimney-corner is really a witch, and that at midnight, when the storm is high, she steals away to the ruined keep, where the spirits of the dead wait spellbound for the word that shall waken them. In all scenes of impish revelry cats play a prominent part, although occasionally, by virtue of their dual natures, they serve as barriers against the powers of evil. There is the old story of the witch's cat that was grateful to the good girl who gave it some ham to eat, — I may observe here, parenthetically, that I have never known a cat that would touch ham, — and there is the fine bit of Italian folk-lore about the servant maid who, with no other protector than a black cat, ventures to disturb a procession of ghosts on the dreadful Night of the Dead. "It is

well for you that the cat lies in your arms,"
the angry spirit says to her ; " otherwise what
I am, you also would be." The last pale reflex
of a universal tradition I found three years
ago in London, where the bad behavior of the
Westminster cats — proverbially the most dis-
solute and profligate specimens of their race —
has given rise to the pleasant legend of a country house whither these rakish animals retire
for nights of gay festivity, and whence they
return in the early morning, jaded, repentant,
and forlorn.

Of late years there has been a rapid and
promising growth of what disaffected and al-
literative critics call the " cat cult," and poets
and painters vie with one another in celebrat-
ing the charms of this long-neglected pet.
Mr. M. H. Spielmann's beautiful volume in
praise of Madame Henriette Ronner and her
pictures is a treasure upon which many an ardent lover of cats will cast wandering and wistful glances. It is impossible for even the most
disciplined spirit not to yearn over these little
furry darlings, these gentle, mischievous, lazy,
irresistible things. As for Banjo, that dear
and sentimental kitten, with his head on one

side like Lydia Languish, and a decorous
melancholy suffusing his splendid eyes, let any
obdurate scorner of the race look at his loveli-
ness and be converted. Mrs. Graham R. Tomson's pretty anthology, " Concerning Cats,"
is another step in the right direction; a dainty
volume of selections from French and English
verse, where we may find old favorites like
Cowper's " Retired Cat " and Calverly's " Sad
Memories," graceful epitaphs on departed pussies, some delightful poems from Baudelaire,
and three, no less delightful, from the pen of
Mrs. Tomson herself, whose preface, or " fore-
word," is enough to win for her at once the
friendship and sympathy of the elect.   The
book, while it contains a good deal that might
well have been omitted, is necessarily a small
one; for poets, English poets especially, have
just begun to sing the praises of the cat, as
they have for generations sung the praises of
the horse and dog.   Nevertheless, all English
literature, and all the literatures of every land,
are full of charming allusions to this friendly
animal, — allusions the brevity of which only
enhances their value.   Those two delicious
lines of Herrick's, for example, —

"And the brisk mouse may feast herself with crumbs,
Till that the green-eyed kitling comes," —

are worth the whole of Wordsworth's solemn
poem, "The Kitten and the Falling Leaves."
What did Wordsworth know of the innate
vanity, the affectation and coquetry, of kitten-
hood? He saw the little beast gamboling on
the wall, and he fancied her as innocent as she
looked, — as though any living creature *could*
be as innocent as a kitten looks! With touching simplicity, he believed her all unconscious
of the admiration she was exciting : —

"What would little Tabby care
For the plaudits of the crowd ?
Over happy to be proud,
Over wealthy in the treasure
Of her own exceeding pleasure! "

Ah, the arrant knavery of that kitten! The
tiny impostor, showing off her best tricks, and
feigning to be occupied exclusively with her
own infantile diversion! We can see her now,
prancing and paddling after the leaves, and
all the while peeping out of "the tail o' her
ee" at the serene poet and philosopher, and
waving her naughty tail in glee over his confidence and condescension.

Heine's pretty lines, —

"And close beside me the cat sits purring,
  Warming her paws at the cheery gleam ;
The flames keep flitting, and flicking, and whirring;
  My mind is wrapped in a realm of dream," —

find their English echo in the letter Shelley
writes to Peacock, describing, half wistfully,
the shrines of the Penates, "whose hymns
are the purring of kittens, the hissing of kettles, the long talks over the past and dead, the
laugh of children, the warm wind of summer
filling the quiet house, and the pelting storm
of winter struggling in vain for entrance."
How incomplete would these pictures be, how
incomplete is any fireside sketch, without the
purring kitten or drowsy cat !

"The queen I am o' that cozy place;
  As wi' ilka paw I dicht my face,
  I sing an' purr wi' mickle grace."

This is the sphinx of the hearthstone, the little
god of domesticity, whose presence turns a
house into a home. Even the chilly desolation
of a hotel may be rendered endurable by these
affable and discriminating creatures; for one
of them, as we know, once welcomed Sir Walter Scott, and softened for him the unfamiliar

and unloved surroundings. "There are no
dogs in the hotel where I lodge," he writes to
Abbotsford from London, "but a tolerably
conversable cat *who* eats a mess of cream with
me in the morning." Of course it did, the
wise and lynx-eyed beast! I make no doubt
that, day after day and week after week, that
cat had wandered superbly amid the common
throng of lodgers, showing favor to none, and
growing cynical and disillusioned by constant
contact with a crowd. Then, one morning, it
spied the noble, rugged face which neither man
nor beast could look upon without loving, and
forthwith tendered its allegiance on the spot.
Only "tolerably conversable" it was, this
reserved and town-bred animal; less urbane
because less happy than the much-respected
retainer at Abbotsford, Master Hinse of Hinse-
feld, whom Sir Walter called his friend. "Ah,
mon grand ami, vous avez tué mon autre grand
ami!" he sighed, when the huge hound Nim-
rod ended poor Hinse's placid career. And if
Scott sometimes seems to disparage cats, as
when he unkindly compares Oliver-le-Dain to
one, in "Quentin Durward," he atones for
such indignity by the use of the little pronoun

"who" when writing of the London puss.
My own habit is to say "who" on similar
occasions, and I am glad to have so excellent
an authority.

It were an endless though a pleasant task to
recount all that has been said, and well said,
in praise of the cat by those who have rightly
valued her companionship. M. Loti's Moumoutte Blanche and Moumoutte Chinoise
are well known and widely beloved, and M.
Théophile Gautier's charming pages are too
familiar for comment. Who has not read with
delight of the Black and White Dynasties
that for so long ruled with gentle sway over
his hearth and heart; of Madame Théophile,
who thought the parrot was a green chicken;
of Don Pierrot de Navarre, who deeply resented
his master's staying out late at night; of the
graceful and fastidious Séraphita; the glut-
tonous Enjolras; the acute Bohemian, Ga-
vroche; the courteous and well-mannered Epo-
nine, who received M. Gautier's guests in the
drawing-room and dined at his table, taking
each course as it was served, and restraining
any rude distaste for food not to her fancy.
"Her place was laid without a knife and fork,

indeed, but with a glass, and she went regularly through dinner, from soup to dessert, awaiting her turn to be helped, and behaving with a quiet propriety which most children might imitate with advantage. At the first stroke of the bell she would appear, and when I came into the dining-room she would be at her post, upright on her chair, her forepaws on the edge of the tablecloth; and she would present her smooth forehead to be kissed, like a well-bred little girl who was affectionately polite to relatives and old people."

I have read this pretty description several times to Agrippina, who is extremely wayward and capricious about her food, rejecting plaintively one day the viands which she has eaten with apparent enjoyment the day before. In fact, the difficulty of catering to her is so well understood by tradesmen that recently, when the housemaid carried her on an errand to the grocery, — Agrippina is very fond of these jaunts and of the admiration she excites, — the grocer, a fatherly man, with cats of his own, said briskly, " Is this the little lady who . eats the biscuits ? " and presented her on the spot with several choice varieties from which

to choose. She is fastidious, too, about the
way in which her meals are served; disliking
any other dishes than her own, which are of
blue-and-white china; requiring that her meat
should be cut up fine and all the fat removed,
and that her morning oatmeal should be well
sugared and creamed. Milk she holds in scorn.
My friends tell me sometimes that it is not
the common custom of cats to receive so much
attention at table, and that it is my fault
Agrippina is so exacting; but such grumblers
fail to take into consideration the marked in-
dividuality that is the charm of every kindly
treated puss. She differs from her sisters as
widely as one woman differs from another,
and reveals varying characteristics of good and
evil, varying powers of intelligence and adap-
tation. She scales splendid heights of virtue,
and, unlike Sir Thomas Browne, is " singular
in offenses." Even those primitive instincts
which we believe all animals hold in common
are lost in acquired ethics and depravity. No
heroism could surpass that of the London cat
who crawled back five times under the stage
of the burning theatre to rescue her litter of
kittens, and, having carried four of them to

safety, perished devotedly with the fifth. On
the other hand, I know of a cat who drowned
her three kittens in a water-butt, for no reason,
apparently, save to be rid of them, and that
she might lie in peace on the hearth rug, — a
murder well planned, deliberate, and cruel.

> " So Tiberius might have sat,
> Had Tiberius been a cat."

Only in her grace and beauty, her love of
comfort, her dignity of bearing, her courteous
reserve, and her independence of character
does puss remain immutable and unchanged.
These are the traits which win for her the
warmest corner by the fire, and the unshaken
regard of those who value her friendship and
aspire to her affection. These are the traits so
subtly suggested by Mrs. Tomson in a sonnet
which every true lover of cats feels in his heart
must have been addressed to his own particular pet : —

> " Half gentle kindliness, and half disdain,
> Thou comest to my call, serenely suave,
> With humming speech and gracious gestures grave,
> In salutation courtly and urbane ;
> Yet must I humble me thy grace to gain,
> For wiles may win thee, but no arts enslave ;

And nowhere gladly thou abidest, save
Where naught disturbs the concord of thy reign.

" Sphinx of my quiet hearth ! who deign'st to dwell
Friend of my toil, companion of mine ease,
Thine is the lore of Ra and Rameses ;
That men forget dost thou remember well, ·
Beholden still in blinking reveries,
With sombre sea-green gaze inscrutable."

THE CHILDREN'S POETS.

Now and then I hear it affirmed by sad-voiced pessimists, whispering in the gloom, that people do not read as much poetry in our day as they did in our grandfathers', that this is distinctly the era of prose, and that the poet is no longer, as Shelley claimed, the unacknowledged legislator of the world. Perhaps these cheerless statements are true, though it would be more agreeable not to believe them. Perhaps, with the exception of Browning, whom we study because he is difficult to understand, and of Shakespeare, whom we read because it is hard to content our souls without him, the poets have slipped away from our crowded lives, and are best known to us through the medium of their reviewers. We are always wandering from the paths of pleasure, and this may be one of our deviations. Yet what matters it, after all, while around us, on every side, in schoolrooms and nurseries, in quiet corners and by cheerful fires, the children are reading poetry? — reading it with a joyous enthusiasm and an absolute surrendering of spirit which we can all remember, but can never feel again. Well might Sainte-Beuve speak bravely of the clear, fine penetration peculiar to childhood. Well might he recall, with wistful sighs, "that instinctive knowledge which afterwards ripens into judgment, but of which the fresh lucidity remains forever unapproached." He knew, as all critics have known, that it is only the child who responds swiftly, pliantly, and unreservedly to the allurements of the imagination. He knew that, when poetry is in question, it is better to feel than to think; and that with the growth of a guarded and disciplined intelligence, straining after the enjoyment which perfection in literary art can give, the first careless rapture of youth fades into a half-remembered dream.

If we are disposed to doubt the love that children bear to poetry, a love concerning which they exhibit a good deal of reticence, let us consider only the alacrity with which they study, for their own delight, the poems

that please them best. How should we fare,
I wonder, if tried by a similar test? How
should we like to sit down and commit to
memory Tennyson's " Œnone, " or " Locksley
Hall," or Byron's apostrophe to the Ocean, or
the battle scene in " Marmion "? Yet I have
known children to whom every word of these
and many other poems was as familiar as the
alphabet; and a great deal more familiar —
thank Heaven! — than the multiplication
table, or the capitals of the United States. A
rightly constituted child may find the paths of
knowledge hopelessly barred by a single page
of geography, or by a single sum in fractions ;
but he will range at pleasure through the
paths of poetry, having the open sesame to
every door. Sir Walter Scott, who was essentially a rightly constituted child, did not even
wait for a formal introduction to his letters,
but managed to learn the ballad of Hardy-
knute before he knew how to read, and went
shouting it around the house, warming his
baby blood to fighting-point, and training
himself in very infancy to voice the splendors
of his manhood. He remembered this ballad,
too, and loved it all his life, reciting it once

with vast enthusiasm to Lord Byron, whose
own unhappy childhood had been softened
and vivified by the same innocent delights.

In truth, the most charming thing about
youth is the tenacity of its impressions. If
we had the time and courage to study a dozen
verses to-day, we should probably forget
eleven of them in a fortnight; but the poetry
we learned as children remains, for the most
part, indelibly fixed in our memories, and
constitutes a little Golden Treasury of our
own, more dear and valuable to us than any
other collection, because it contains only our
chosen favorites, and is always within the reach
of reference. Once, when I was very young, I
asked a girl companion — well known now in
the world of literature — if she did not grow
weary waiting for trains, which were always
late, at the suburban station where she went
to school. " Oh, no," was the cheerful reply.
" If I have no book, and there is no one
here to talk with, I walk up and down the
platform and think over the poetry that I
know." Admirable occupation for an idle
minute ! Even the tedium of railway traveling loses half its horrors if one can withdraw

at pleasure into the society of the poets and, soothed by their gentle and harmonious voices, forget the irksome recurrence of familiar things.

It has been often demonstrated, and as often forgotten, that children do not need to have poetry written down to their intellectual level, and do not love to see the stately Muse ostentatiously bending to their ear. In the matter of prose, it seems necessary for them to have a literature of their own, over which they linger willingly for a little while, as though in the sunny antechamber of a king. But in the golden palace of the poets there is no period of probation, there is no enforced attendance upon petty things. The clear-eyed children go straight to the heart of the mystery, and recognize in the music of words, in the enduring charm of metrical quality, an element of never-ending delight. When to this simple sensuous pleasure is added the enchantment of poetic images, lovely and veiled and dimly understood, then the delight grows sweeter and keener, the child's soul flowers into a conscious love of poetry, and one lifelong source of happiness is gained.

But it is never through infantine or juvenile
verses that the end is reached. There is no
poet dearer to the young than Tennyson, and
it was not the least of his joys to know that
all over the English-speaking world children
were tuning their hearts to the music of his
lines, were dreaming vaguely and rapturously
over the beauty he revealed. Therefore the
insult seemed greater and more wanton when
this beloved idol of our nurseries deliberately
offered to his eager audience such anxiously
babyish verses as those about Minnie and
Winnie, and the little city maiden who goes
straying among the flowers. Is there in
Christendom a child who wants to be told by
one of the greatest of poets that

> " Minnie and Winnie
>   Slept in a shell ; "

that the shell was pink within and silver without ; and that

> " Sounds of the great sea
>   Wandered about.
>
> " Two bright stars
>   Peep'd into the shell.
> ' What are they dreaming of ?
>   Who can tell ? ' "

> " Started a green linnet
> Out of the croft ;
> ' Wake, little ladies,
> The sun is aloft.' "

It is not in these tones that poetry speaks to the childish soul, though it is too often in this fashion that the poet strives to adjust himself to what he thinks is the childish standard. He lowers his sublime head from the stars, and pipes with painstaking flatness on a little reed, while the children wander far away, and listen breathlessly to older and dreamier strains.

> " She left the web, she left the loom,
> She made three paces thro' the room,
> She saw the water-lily bloom,
> She saw the helmet and the plume,
>   She look'd down to Camelot,
> Out flew the web and floated wide ;
> The mirror crack'd from side to side ;
> ' The curse is come upon me,' cried
>   The Lady of Shalott."

Here is the mystic note that childhood loves, and here, too, is the sweet constraint of linked rhymes that makes music for its ears. How many of us can remember well our early joy in this poem, which was but as another and

more exquisite fairy tale, ranking fitly with
Andersen's "Little Mermaid," and "Un-
dine," and all sad stories of unhappy lives!
And who shall forget the sombre passion of
" Oriana," of those wailing verses that rang
through our little hearts like the shrill sob-
bing of winter storms, of that strange tragedy
that oppressed us more with fear than pity!

> " When the long dun wolds are ribb'd with snow,
>   And loud the Norland whirlwinds blow,
>   Oriana,
>   Alone I wander to and fro,
>   Oriana."

If any one be inclined to think that children
must understand poetry in order to appreciate
and enjoy it, that one enchanted line, —

> " When the long dun wolds are ribb'd with snow," —

should be sufficient to undeceive him forever.
The spell of those finely chosen words lies in
the shadowy and half-seen picture they convey, — a picture with indistinct outlines, as of
an unknown land, where the desolate spirit
wanders moaning in the gloom. The whole
poem is inexpressibly alluring to an imaginative child, and its atmosphere of bleak despondency darkens suddenly into horror at

the breaking off of the last line from visions of the grave and of peaceful death, —

> " I hear the roaring of the sea,
> Oriana."

The same grace of indistinctness, though linked with a gentler mood and with a softer music, makes the lullaby in " The Princess " a lasting delight to children, while the pretty cradle-song in " Sea Dreams," beginning, —

> " What does little birdie say
> In her nest at peep of day ? "

has never won their hearts. Its motive is too apparent, its nursery flavor too pronounced. It has none of the condescension of " Minnie and Winnie," and grown people can read it with pleasure ; but a simple statement of obvious truths, or a simple line of obvious reasoning, however dexterously narrated in prose or verse, has not the art to hold a youthful soul in thrall.

If it be a matter of interest to know what poets are most dear to the children around us, to the ordinary " apple-eating " little boys and girls for whom we are hardly brave enough to predict a shining future, it is delightful to be told by favorite authors and

by well-loved men of letters what poets first
bewitched their ardent infant minds. It is
especially pleasant to have Mr. Andrew Lang
admit us a little way into his confidence, and
confess to us that he disliked " Tam O'Shan-
ter " when his father read it aloud to him; pre-
ferring, very sensibly, " to take my warlocks
and bogies with great seriousness." Of course
he did, and the sympathies of all children are
with him in his choice. The ghastly details
of that witches' Sabbath are far beyond a
child's limited knowledge of demonology and
the Scotch dialect. Tam's escape and Mag-
gie's final catastrophe seem like insults offered
to the powers of darkness; only the humor of
the situation is apparent, and humor is seldom,
to the childish mind, a desirable element of
poetry. Not all the spirit of Caldecott's illustrations can make " John Gilpin " a real favorite in our nurseries, while " The Jackdaw of
Rheims " is popular simply because children,
being proof against cynicism, accept the story
as it is told, with much misplaced sympathy
for the thievish bird, and many secret rejoi-
cings over his restoration to grace and feath-
ers. As for " The Pied Piper of Hamelin,"

its humor is swallowed up in tragedy, and the
terror of what is to come helps little readers
over such sad stumbling-blocks as

> "So munch on, crunch on, take your nuncheon,
> Breakfast, dinner, supper, luncheon!"

lines which are every whit as painful to their
ears as to ours. I have often wondered how
the infant Southeys and Coleridges, that
bright-eyed group of alert and charming children, all afire with romantic impulses, received
"The Cataract of Lodore," when papa Southey
condescended to read it in the schoolroom.
What well-bred efforts to appear pleased and
grateful! What secret repulsion to a senseless
clatter of words, as remote from the silvery
sweetness, the cadenced music of falling waters,
as from the unalterable requirements of poetic
art!

> "And moreover he tasked me
> To tell him in rhyme."

Ah! unwise little son, to whose rash request
generations of children have owed the presence,
in readers and elocution-books and volumes of
"Select Lyrics for the Nursery," of those
hated and hateful verses.

"Poetry came to me with Sir Walter Scott,"

says Mr. Lang; with "Marmion," and the "Last Minstrel," and "The Lady of the Lake," read "for the twentieth time," and ever with fresh delight. Poetry came to Scott with Shakespeare, studied rapturously by fire-light in his mother's dressing-room, when all the household thought him fast asleep, and with Pope's translation of the Iliad, that royal road over which the Muse has stepped, smiling, into many a boyish heart. Poetry came to Pope — poor little lame lad — with Spenser's "Faerie Queene;" with the brave adventures of strong, valiant knights, who go forth, un-blemished and unfrighted, to do battle with dragons and "Paynims cruel." And so the links of the magic chain are woven, and child hands down to child the spell that holds the centuries together. I cannot bear to hear the unkind things which even the most tolerant of critics are wont to say about Pope's "Iliad," remembering as I do how many boys have re-ceived from its pages their first poetic stimulus, their first awakening to noble things. What a charming picture we have of Coleridge, a feeble, petulant child tossing with fever on his little bed, and of his brother Francis stealing

up, in defiance of all orders, to sit by his side
and read him Pope's translation of Homer.
The bond that drew these boys together was
forged in such breathless moments and in such
mutual pleasures ; for Francis, the handsome,
spirited sailor lad, who climbed trees, and
robbed orchards, and led all dangerous sports,
had little in common with his small, silent, pre-
cocious brother. " Frank had a violent love
of beating me," muses Coleridge, in a tone of
mild complaint (and no wonder, we think, for
a more beatable child than Samuel Taylor it
would have been hard to find). " But whenever that was superseded by any humor or
circumstance, he was very fond of me, and used
to regard me with a strange mixture of admiration and contempt." More contempt than admiration, probably ; yet was all resentment
forgotten, and all unkindness at an end, while
one boy read to the other the story of Hector
and Patroclus, and of great Ajax, with sorrow
in his heart, pacing round his dead comrade,
as a tawny lioness paces round her young
when she sees the hunters coming through
the woods. As a companion picture to this
we have little Dante Gabriel Rossetti playing

Othello in the nursery, and so carried away by
the passionate impulse of these lines, —

> "In Aleppo once,
> Where a malignant and a turban'd Turk
> Beat a Venetian and traduced the state,
> I took by the throat the circumcised dog,
> And smote him, thus," —

that he struck himself fiercely on the breast
with an iron chisel, and fainted under the
blow. We can hardly believe that Shakespeare is beyond the mental grasp of childhood,
when Scott, at seven, crept out of bed on
winter nights to read "King Henry IV.," and
Rossetti, at nine, was overwhelmed by the
agony of Othello's remorse.

On the other hand, there are writers, and
very brilliant writers, too, whose early lives
appear to have been undisturbed by such
keenly imaginative pastimes, and for whom
there are no well-loved and familiar figures
illumined forever in "that bright, clear, undying light that borders the edge of the oblivion
of infancy." Count Tolstoi confesses himself
to have been half hurt, half puzzled, by his
fellow-students at the University of Mos-
cow, who seemed to him so coarse and inele-

gant, and yet who had read and enjoyed so
much. "Pushkin and Zhukovsky were literature to them," he says wistfully, "and not, as
to me, little books in yellow bindings which I
had studied as a child." But how, one wonders, could Pushkin have remained merely a
"little book in yellow binding" to any boy
who had had the happiness of studying him as
a child? Pushkin is the Russian Byron, and
embodies in his poems the same spirit of restless discontent, of dejected languor, of passionate revolt; not revolt against the Tsar,
which is a limited and individual judgment,
but revolt against the bitter penalties of life,
which is a sentiment common to the youth of
all nations and of every age. Yet there are
Englishmen who have no word save that of
scorn for Byron, and I feel uncertain whether
such critics ever enjoyed the privilege of being
boys at all. If to George Meredith's composed
and complacent mind there strays any wanton
recollection of young, impetuous days, how
can he write with pen of gall these worse than
churlish lines on Manfred? —

> "Projected from the bilious Childe,
> This clatterjaw his foot could set

On Alps, without a breast beguiled
To glow in shedding rascal sweat.
Somewhere about his grinder teeth
He mouthed of thoughts that grilled beneath,
And summoned Nature to her feud
With bile and buskin attitude."

There is more of this pretty poem, but I have quoted as much as my own irascibility can bear. I, at least, have been a child, and have spent some of my childhood's happiest hours with Manfred on the Alps; and have with him beheld

"the tall pines dwindled as to shrubs
In dizziness of distance,"

and have believed with all a child's sincerity in his remorseful gloom :—

"for I have ceased
To justify my deeds unto myself—
The last infirmity of evil."

Every line is inexpressibly dear to me now, recalling, as it does, the time " when I was in my father's house, and my path ran down with butter and honey." Once more I see the big, bare, old-fashioned parlor, to dust which was my daily task, my dear mother having striven long and vainly to teach my idle little hands some useful housewifely accomplishment. In

one corner stood a console-table, with chilly
Parian ornaments on top, and underneath a
pile of heavy books; Wordsworth, Moore, the
poems of Frances Sargent Osgood, — no lack
of variety here, — " The Lady of the Lake,"
and Byron in an embossed brown binding, with
closely printed double columns, well calculated
to dim the keenest sight in Christendom. Not
that mysterious and malignant mountain which
rose frowning from the sea, and drew all ships
shattered to its feet, was more irresistible in
its attraction than this brown, bulky Byron.
I could not pass it by! My dusting never got
beyond the table where it lay; but sitting
crumpled on the floor, with the enchanted
volume on my lap, I speedily. forgot everything in the world save only the wandering
Childe,

    " Who ne in virtue's ways did take delight,"

or " The Corsair," or " Mazeppa," or " Manfred," best loved of that dark group. Perhaps
Byron is not considered wholesome reading for
little girls in these careful days when expur-
gated editions of " The Vicar of Wakefield "
and " Paul and Virginia " find favor in our
nurseries. On this score I have no defense to

offer, and I am not proposing the poet as a safe text-book for early youth; but having never been told that there was such a thing as forbidden fruit in literature, I was spared at least that alert curiosity concerning it which is one of the most unpleasant results of our present guarded system. Moreover, we have Goethe's word for it that Byron is not as immoral as the newspapers, and certainly he is more agreeable reading. I do sincerely believe that if part of his attraction for the young lies in what Mr. Pater calls "the grieved dejection, the endless regret," which to the undisciplined soul sounds like the true murmur of life, a better part lies in his large grasp of nature, — not nature in her minute and lovely detail, but in her vast outlines, her salient features, her solemn majesty and strength. Crags and misty mountain tops, storm-swept skies and the blue bosom of the restless deep, — these are the aspects of nature that childhood prizes, and loves to hear described in vigorous verse. The pink-tipped daisy, the yellow primrose, and the freckled nest-eggs

" Hatching in the hawthorn-tree "

belong to a late stage of development. Eugénie de Guérin, who recognized as clearly as Sainte-Beuve the " fine penetration " peculiar to children, and who regarded them ever with half-wistful, half-wondering delight, has written some very charming suggestions about the kind of poetry, " pure, fresh, joyous, and delicate," which she considered proper food for these highly idealized little people, — " angels upon earth." The only discouraging part of her pretty pleading is her frank admission that — in French literature, at least — there is no such poetry as she describes, which shows how hard it is to conciliate an exclusive theory of excellence. She endeavored sincerely, in her " Infantines," to remedy this defect, to " speak to childhood in its own language ; " and her verses on " Joujou, the Angel of the Playthings," are quaintly conceived and full of gentle fancies. No child is strongly moved, or taught the enduring delight of song, by such lines as these, but most children will take a genuine pleasure in the baby angel who played with little Abel under the myrtle-trees, who made the first doll and blew the first bubble, and who finds a friend in every tiny boy and girl born into this

big gray world. Strange to say, he has his
English counterpart in Mr. Robert Louis
Stevenson's "Unseen Playmate," that shadowy
companion whose home is the cave dug by
childish hands, and who is ready to share all
games in the most engaging spirit of accom-
modation.

> " 'T is he, when you play with your soldiers of tin,
>   That sides with the Frenchmen, and never can win; "

a touch of combative veracity which brings us
down at once from Mademoiselle de Guérin's
fancy flights to the real playground, where
real children, very faintly resembling " angels
upon earth," are busy with mimic warfare.
Mr. Stevenson is one of the few poets whose
verses, written especially for the nursery, have
found their way straight into little hearts.
His charming style, his quick, keen sympathy,
and the ease with which he enters into that
brilliant world of imagination wherein children habitually dwell, make him their natural
friend and minstrel. If some of the rhymes
in "A Child's Garden of Verses" seem a trifle
bald and babyish, even these are guiltless
of condescension; while others, like "Travel,"
"Shadow March," and "The Land of Story-

Books," are instinct with poetic life. I can only regret that a picture so faultless in detail as "Shadow March," where we see the crawling darkness peer through the window pane, and hear the beating of the little boy's heart as he creeps fearfully up the stair, should be marred at its close by a single line of false imagery : —

> "All the wicked shadows coming, tramp, tramp, tramp,
>   With the black night overhead."

So fine an artist as Mr. Stevenson must know that shadows do not tramp, and that the recurrence of a short, vigorous word which tells so admirably in Scott's " William and Helen," and wherever the effect of sound combined with motion is to be conveyed, is sadly out of place in describing the ghostly things that glide with horrible noiselessness at the feet of the frightened lad. Children, moreover, are keenly alive to the value and the suggestiveness of terms. A little eight-year-old girl of my acquaintance, who was reciting " Lord Ullin's Daughter," stopped short at these lines, —

> "Adown the glen rode armed men,
>   Their trampling sounded nearer," —

and called out excitedly, " Don't you hear the

horses?" She, at least, heard them as if with the swift apprehension of fear, heard them loud above the sounds of winds and waters, and rendered her unconscious tribute of praise to the sympathetic selection of words.

There is, as we know, a great deal of poetry written every year for childish readers. Some of it makes its appearance in Christmas books, which are so beautifully bound and illustrated that the little foolish, feeble verses are forgiven, and in fact forgotten, ignored altogether amid more important accessories. Better poems than these are published in children's periodicals, where they form a notable feature, and are, I dare say, read by the young people whose tastes are catered to in this fashion. Those of us who are familiar with these periodicals — either weeklies or monthlies — are well aware that the verses they offer may be easily divided into three classes. First, mere rhymes and jingles, intended for very little readers, and with which it would be simple churlishness to quarrel. They do not aspire to be poetry, they are sometimes very amusing, and they have an easy swing that is pleasant alike to young ears and old. It must be a hard heart

that does not sympathize with the unlucky and
ill-mated gnome who was

"full of fun and frolic,
But his wife was melancholic;"

or with the small damsel in pigtail and pina-
fore who comforts herself at the piano with
this engaging but dubious maxim : —

"Practicing is good for a good little girl ;
It makes her nose straight, and it makes her hair curl."

The second kind of verse appears to be written
solely for the sake of the accompanying illustration, and is often the work of the illustrator,
who is more at home with his pencil than his
pen. Occasionally it is comic, occasionally
sentimental or descriptive ; for the most part
it is something in this style : —

THE ELF AND THE BUMBLE BEE.

"Oh, bumble bee!
Bumble bee !
Don't fly so near!
Or you will tumble me
Over, I fear."

"Oh, funny elf !
Funny elf !
Don't be alarmed !
I am looking for honey, elf ;
You sha'n't be harmed."

" Then tarry,
           Oh, tarry, bee !
      Fill up your sack ;
      And carry, oh, carry me
      Home on your back." [1]

Now what child will read more than once these
empty little verses (very prettily illustrated)
when it is in his power to turn back to other
sprites that sing in different strains, — to the
fairy who wanders

" Over hill, over dale,
      Thorough bush, thorough briar, "

seeking pearl eardrops for the cowslips' ears ;
or to that softer shape, the music of whose
song, once heard, haunts us forever : —

" Full fathom five thy father lies ;
      Of his bones are coral made ;
      Those are pearls that were his eyes :
      Nothing of him that doth fade
      But doth suffer a sea-change
      Into something rich and strange."

These are the sweet, mysterious echoes of true
fairyland, where Shakespeare and little children wander at their will.

Poems of the third class are intended for
growing girls and boys, and aspire to be

[1] Oliver Herford in *St. Nicholas.*

considered literature. They are well written, as a rule, with a smooth fluency that seems to be the distinguishing gift of our minor verse-makers, who, even when they have least to say, say it with unbroken sweetness and grace. This pretty, easy insignificance is much better adapted to adult readers, who demand little of poets beyond brevity, than to children, who love large issues, real passions, fine emotions, and an heroic attitude in life. Pleasant thoughts couched in pleasant language, trivial details, and photographic bits of description make no lasting appeal to the expansive imagination of a child. Analysis is wasted upon him altogether, because he sees things swiftly, and sees them as a whole. He may disregard fine shading and minute merits, but there are no boundaries to his wandering vision. " Small sciences are the labors of our manhood, but the round universe is the plaything of the boy."

The painful lack of distinction in most of the poetry prepared especially for him chills his fine ardor and dulls his imagination. Subtle verses about moods and tempers, calculated to make healthy little readers emu-

late Miss Martineau's peevish self-sympathy;
melancholy verses about young children who
suffer poverty and disaster; weird and unin-
telligible verses, with all Poe's indistinctness
and none of his music; commonplace verses
about bootblacks and newsboys; descriptive
verses about snowstorms and April showers;
pious verses about infant prigs; — verses of
every kind, all on the same level of agreeable
mediocrity, and all warranted to be so harmless that a baby could hear them without
blushing.   Why, the child who reads "Young
Lochinvar" is richer in that one good and gallant poem than the child who has all these
modern substitutes heaped yearly at his foolish feet.

For the question at issue is not what kind
of poetry is wholesome for children, but what
kind of poetry do children love.   In nineteen
cases out of twenty, that which they love is
good for them, and they can guide themselves
a great deal better than we can hope to guide
them.   I once asked a friend who had spent
many years in teaching little girls and boys
whether her small pupils, when left to their
own discretion, ever chose any of the pretty,

trivial verses out of new books and magazines for study and recitation. She answered, Never. They turned instinctively to the same old favorites she had been listening to so long; to the same familiar poems that their fathers and mothers had probably studied and recited before them. " Hohenlinden," " Glenara," " Lord Ullin's Daughter," " Young Lochinvar," " Rosabelle," " To Lucasta, on going to the Wars," the lullaby from " The Princess," " Lady Clara Vere de Vere," " Annabel Lee," Longfellow's translation of " The Castle by the Sea," and " The Skeleton in Armor," — these are the themes of which children never weary; these are the songs that are sung forever in their secret Paradise of Delights. The little volumes containing such tried and proven friends grow shabby with much handling; and I have seen them marked all over with mysterious crosses and dots and stars, each of which denoted the exact degree of affection which the child bore to the poem thus honored and approved. I can fancy Mr. Lang's " Blue Poetry Book " fairly covered with such badges of distinction; for never before has any selection of poems appealed so clearly and insistently to childish tastes and hearts. When I turn over its pages, I feel as if the children of England must have brought their favorite songs to Mr. Lang, and prayed, each one, that his own darling might be admitted, — as if they must have forced his choice into their chosen channels. Its only rival in the field, Palgrave's "Children's Treasury of English Song," is edited with such nice discrimination, such critical reserve, that it is well-nigh flawless, — a triumph of delicacy and good taste. But much that childhood loves is necessarily excluded from a volume so small and so carefully considered. The older poets, it is true, are generously treated, — Herrick, especially, makes a braver show than he does in Mr. Lang's collection; and there are plenty of beautiful ballads, some of which, like "The Lass of Lochroyan," we miss sorely from the pages of the "Blue Poetry Book." On the other hand, where, in Mr. Palgrave's "Treasury," are those lovely snatches of song familiar to our earliest years, and which we welcome individually with a thrill of pleasure, as Mr. Lang shows them to us once more? — "Rose Aylmer," "County Guy," "Proud Maisie,"

" How Sleep the Brave," " Nora's Vow," —
the delight of my own childhood, — the pathetic " Farewell," —

> "It was a' for our rightfu' King,
> We left fair Scotland's strand;
> It was a' for our rightfu' King,
> We e'er saw Irish land," —

and Hood's silvery little verses beginning, —

> "A lake and a fairy boat
> To sail in the moonlight clear, —
> And merrily we would float
> From the dragons that watch us here!"

All these and many more are gathered safely
into this charming volume. Nothing we long
to see appears to be left out, except, indeed,
Waller's " Go, Lovely Rose," and Herrick's
" Night Piece," both of them very serious omis-
sions. It seems strange to find seven of Edgar
Poe's poems in a collection which excludes the
" Night Piece," so true a favorite with all girl
children, and a favorite that, once rightfully
established, can never be thrust from our affections. As for Praed's " Red Fisherman," Mr.
Lang has somewhere recorded his liking for
this " sombre " tale, which, I think, embodies
everything that a child ought not to love. It

is the only poem in the book that I wish elsewhere; but perhaps this is a perverse prejudice
on my part. There may be little readers to
whom its savage cynicism and gloom carry a
pleasing terror, like that which oppressed my
infant soul as I lingered with Goodman Brown
in the awful witch-haunted forest where Haw-
thorne has shown us the triumph of evil things.
" It is his excursions into the unknown world
which the child enjoys," says Mr. Lang; and
how shall we set a limit to his wanderings! He
journeys far with careless, secure footsteps;
and for him the stars sing in their spheres,
and fairies dance in the moonlight, and the
hoarse clashing of arms rings bravely from
hard-won fields, and lovers fly together under
the stormy skies. He rides with Lochinvar,
and sails with Sir Patrick Spens into the north-
ern seas, and chases the red deer with Allen-a-
Dale, and stands by Marmion's side in the
thick of the ghastly fray. He has given his
heart to Helen of Troy, and to the Maid of
Saragossa, and to the pale child who met her
death on the cruel Gordon spears, and to the
lady with yellow hair who knelt moaning by
Barthram's bier. His friends are bold Robin

Hood, and Lancelot du Lac, and the white-
plumed Henry of Navarre, and the princely
scapegrace who robbed the robbers to make
" laughter for a month, and a good jest forever." A lordly company these, and seldom
to be found in the gray walks of middle age.
Robin Hood dwells not on the Stock Exchange,
and Prince Hal dare not show his laughing
face before societies for leveling thrones and
reorganizing the universe. We adults pass
our days, alas, in the Town of Stupidity, —
abhorred of Bunyan's soul, — and our com-
panions are Mr. Worldly Wiseman, and Mr.
Despondency, and Mr. Want-wit, still scrub-
bing his Ethiopian, and Mr. Feeble-mind, and
the " deplorable young woman named Dull."
But it is better to be young, and to see the
golden light of romance in the skies, and to
kiss the white feet of Helen, as she stands like
a star on the battlements. It is better to follow Hector to the fight, and Guinevere to the
sad cloisters of Almesbury, and the Ancient
Mariner to that silent sea where the death-
fires gleam by night. Even to us who have
made these magic voyages in our childhood
there comes straying, at times, a pale reflection

of that early radiance, a faint, sweet echo
of that early song. Then the streets of the
Town of Stupidity grow soft to tread, and Falstaff's great laugh frightens Mr. Despondency
into a shadow. Then Madeline smiles on us
under the wintry moonlight, and Porphyro
steals by with strange sweets heaped in bas-
kets of wreathed silver. Then we know that
with the poets there is perpetual youth, and
that for us, as for the child dreaming in the
firelight, the shining casements open upon
fairyland.

THE PRAISES OF WAR.

WHEN the world was younger and perhaps merrier, when people lived more and thought less, and when the curious subtleties of an advanced civilization had not yet turned men's heads with conceit of their own enlightening progress from simple to serious things, poets had two recognized sources of inspiration, which were sufficient for themselves and for their unexacting audiences. They sang of love and they sang of war, of fair women and of brave men, of keen youthful passions and of the dear delights of battle. Sweet Rosamonde lingers " in Woodstocke bower," and Sir Cauline wrestles with the Eldridge knighte; Annie of Lochroyan sails over the roughening seas, and Lord Percy rides gayly to the Cheviot hills with fifteen hundred bowmen at his back. It did not occur to the thick-headed generation who first listened to the ballad of " Chevy Chace " to hint that the game was hardly worth the candle, or that poaching on a large scale was as reprehensible ethically as poaching on a little one. This sort of insight was left for the nineteenth-century philosopher, and the nineteenth-century moralist. In earlier, easier days, the last thing that a poet troubled himself about was a defensible motive for the battle in which his soul exulted. IIis business was to describe the fighting, not to justify the fight, which would have been a task of pure supererogation in that truculent age. Fancy trying to justify Kinmont Willie or Johnie of Braedislee, instead of counting the hard knocks they give and the stout men they lay low!

> " Johnie 's set his back against an aik,
>   His foot against a stane ;
>   And he has slaiu the Seven Foresters, —
>   He has slain them a' but ane."

The last echo of this purely irresponsible spirit may be found in the " War Song of Dinas Vawr," where Peacock, always three hundred years behind his time, sings of slaughter with a bellicoso cheerfulness which only his admirable versification can excuse : —

> " The mountain sheep are sweeter,
>   But the valley sheep are fatter ;

> We therefore deemed it meeter
> To carry off the latter.
> We made an expedition;
> We met an host and quelled it;
> We forced a strong position,
> And killed the men who held it."

There is not even a lack of food at home —
the old traditional dinner of spurs — to war-
rant this foray. There is no hint of necessity
for the harriers, or consideration for the har-
ried.

> " We brought away from battle,
> And much their land bemoaned them,
> Two thousand head of cattle,
> And the head of him who owned them:
> Ednyfed, King of Dyfed,
> His head was borne before us;
> His wine and beasts supplied our feasts,
> And his overthrow our chorus."

It is impossible to censure a deed so irresistibly
narrated; but if the lines were a hair-breadth
less mellifluous, I think we should call this a
very barbarous method of campaigning.

When the old warlike spirit was dying out
of English verse, when poets had begun to
meditate and moralize, to interpret nature and
to counsel man, the good gods gave to England, as a link with the days that were dead,

Sir Walter Scott, who sang, as no Briton before or since has ever sung, of battlefields and the hoarse clashing of arms, of brave deeds and midnight perils, of the outlaw riding by Brignall banks, and the trooper shaking his silken bridle reins upon the river shore : —

> " Adieu for evermore,
>   My love !
> And adieu for evermore."

These are not precisely the themes which enjoy unshaken popularity to-day, — " the poet of battles fares ill in modern England," says Sir Francis Doyle, — and as a consequence there are many people who speak slightingly of Scott's poetry, and who appear to claim for themselves some inscrutable superiority by so doing. They give you to understand, without putting it too coarsely into words, that they are beyond that sort of thing, but that they liked it very well as children, and are pleased if you enjoy it still. There is even a class of unfortunates who, through no apparent fault of their own, have ceased to take delight in Scott's novels, and who manifest a curious indignation because the characters in them go ahead and do things, instead of thinking and

talking about them, which is the present
approved fashion of evolving fiction. Why,
what time have the good people in " Quentin
Durward " for speculation and chatter ? The
rush of events carries them irresistibly into
action. They plot, and fight, and run away,
and scour the country, and meet with so many
adventures, and perform so many brave and
cruel deeds, that they have no chance for introspection and the joys of analysis. Naturally, those writers who pride themselves upon
making a story out of nothing, and who are
more concerned with excluding material than
with telling their tales, have scant liking for
Sir Walter, who thought little and prated not
at all about the " art of fiction," but used the
subjects which came to hand with the instinctive and unhesitating skill of a great artist.
The battles in " Quentin Durward " and " Old
Mortality " are, I think, as fine in their way as
the battle of Flodden ; and Flodden, says Mr.
Lang, is the finest fight on record, — " better
even than the stand of Aias by the ships in
the Iliad, better than the slaying of the Wooers
in the Odyssey."

The ability to carry us whither he would, to

show us whatever he pleased, and to stir our
hearts' blood with the story of

> "old, unhappy, far-off things,
> And battles long ago,"

was the especial gift of Scott, — of the man
whose sympathies were as deep as life itself,
whose outlook was as wide as the broad
bosom of the earth he trod on. He believed
in action, and he delighted in describing it.
"The thinker's voluntary death in life" was
not, for him, the power that moves the world,
but rather deeds, — deeds that make history
and that sing themselves forever. He honestly
felt himself to be a much smaller man than
Wellington. He stood abashed in the presence of the soldier who had led large issues
and controlled the fate of nations. He would
have been sincerely amused to learn from
"Robert Elsmere" — what a delicious thing
it is to contemplate Sir Walter reading
"Robert Elsmere" ! — that "the decisive
events of the world take place in the intellect."
The decisive events of the world, Scott held
to take place in the field of action; on the
plains of Marathon and Waterloo rather than
in the brain tissues of William Godwin. He

knew what befell Athens when she could put
forward no surer defense against Philip of
Macedon than the most brilliant orations ever
written in praise of freedom. It was better,
he probably thought, to argue as the English
did, "in platoons." The schoolboy who fought
with the heroic "Green-Breeks" in the streets
of Edinburgh; the student who led the Tory
youths in their gallant struggle with the riotous Irishmen, and drove them with stout cud-
geling out of the theatre they had disgraced;
the man who, broken in health and spirit, was
yet blithe and ready to back his quarrel with
Gourgaud by giving that gentleman any satisfaction he desired, was consistent throughout
with the simple principles of a bygone generation. " It is clear to me," he writes in his journal, "that what is least forgiven in a man of
any mark or likelihood is want of that article
blackguardly called *pluck*. All the fine qualities of genius cannot make amends for it.
We are told the genius of poets especially
is irreconcilable with this species of gren-
adier accomplishment. If so, *quel chien de
génie !* "

Quel chien de génie indeed, and far beyond

the compass of Scott, who, amid the growing
sordidness and seriousness of an industrial
and discontented age, struck a single resonant
note that rings in our hearts to-day like the
echo of good and joyous things : —

> "Sound, sound the clarion, fill the fife!
>   To all the sensual world proclaim,
>   One crowded hour of glorious life
>   Is worth an age without a name."

The same sentiments are put, it may be remembered, into admirable prose when Graham of
Claverhouse expounds to Henry Morton his
views on living and dying. At present, Philosophy and Philanthropy between them are
hustling poor Glory into a small corner of the
field. Even to the soldier, we are told, it
should be a secondary consideration, or perhaps no consideration at all, his sense of
duty being a sufficient stay. But Scott, like
Homer, held somewhat different views, and
absolutely declined to let " that jade Duty "
have everything her own way. It is the plain
duty of Blount and Eustace to stay by Clare's
side and guard her as they were bidden, instead
of which they rush off, with Sir Walter's tacit
approbation, to the fray.

"No longer Blount the view could bear:
  'By heaven and all its saints ! I swear
    I will not see it lost !
  Fitz-Eustace, you with Lady Clare
  May bid your beads and patter prayer, —
    I gallop to the host.' "

It was this cheerful acknowledgment of human nature as a large factor in life which gave to Scott his genial sympathy with brave, imperfect men ; which enabled him to draw with true and kindly art such soldiers as Le Balafré, and Dugald Dalgetty, and William of Deloraine. Le Balafré, indeed, with his thick-headed loyalty, his conceit of his own wisdom, his unswerving, almost unconscious courage, his readiness to risk his neck for a bride, and his reluctance to marry her, is every whit as veracious as if he were the over-analyzed child of realism, instead of one of the many minor characters thrust with wanton prodigality into the pages of a romantic novel.

Alone among modern poets, Scott sings Homerically of strife. Others have caught the note, but none have upheld it with such sustained force, such clear and joyous resonance. Macaulay has fire and spirit, but he is always too rhetorical, too declamatory, for real emotion.

He stirs brave hearts, it is true, and the finest
tribute to his eloquence was paid by Mrs.
Browning, who said she could not read the
" Lays " lying down ; they drew her irresistibly
to her feet.   But when Macaulay sings of Lake
Regillus, I do not see the battle swim before
my eyes.   I see — whether I want to or not —
a platform, and the poet's own beloved schoolboy declaiming with appropriate gestures those
glowing and vigorous lines.   When Scott sings
of Flodden, I stand wraith-like in the thickest
of the fray.   I know how the Scottish ranks
waver and reel before the charge of Stanley's
men, how Tunstall's stainless banner sweeps
the field, and how, in the gathering gloom,

> " The stubborn spearmen still made good
>   Their dark impenetrable wood,
>   Each stepping where his comrade stood,
>   The instant that he fell."

There is none of this noble simplicity in the
somewhat dramatic ardor of Horatius, or in the
pharisaical flavor, inevitable perhaps, but not
the less depressing, of Naseby and Ivry, which
read a little like old Kaiser William's war
dispatches turned into verse.   Better a thousand
times are the splendid swing, the captivating

enthusiasm of Drayton's "Agincourt," which hardly a muck-worm could hear unstirred. Reading it, we are as keen for battle as were King Harry's soldiers straining at the leash. The ardor for strife, the staying power of quiet courage, all are here ; and here, too, a felicity of language that makes each noble name a trumpet blast of defiance, a fresh incentive to heroic deeds.

> " With Spanish yew so strong,
> Arrows a cloth-yard long,
> That like to serpents stung,
>   Piercing the weather ;
> None from his fellow starts,
> But playing manly parts,
> And like true English hearts,
>   Stuck close together.
>   .   .   .   .   .   .
> " Warwick in blood did wade,
> Oxford the foe invade,
> And cruel slaughter made,
>   Still as they ran up ;
> Suffolk his axe did ply,
> Beaumont and Willoughby
> Bare them right doughtily,
>   Ferrers and Fanhope.
>
> " Upon Saint Crispin's day
> Fought was this noble fray,
> Which fame did not delay
>   To England to carry ;

> Oh, when shall Englishmen
> With such acts fill a pen,
> Or England breed again
>   Such a King Harry ? ''

Political economists and chilly historians and all long-headed calculating creatures generally may perhaps hint that invading France was no part of England's business, and represented fruitless labor and bloodshed. But this, happily, is not the poet's point of view. He dreams with Hotspur

> '' Of basilisks, of cannon, culverin,
>   Of prisoners' ransom and of soldiers slain,
>   And all the 'currents of a heady fight.''

He hears King Harry's voice ring clearly above the cries and clamors of battle : —

> '' Once more unto the breach, dear friends, once more ;
>   Or close the wall up with our English dead ; ''

and to him the fierce scaling of Harfleur and the field of Agincourt seem not only glorious but righteous things. ''That pure and generous desire to thrash the person opposed to you because he *is* opposed to you, because he is not 'your side,''' which Mr. Saintsbury declares to be the real incentive of all good war songs, hardly permits a too cautious analysis of mo-

tives. Fighting is not a strictly philanthropic
pastime, and its merits are not precisely the
merits of church guilds and college settlements.
Warlike saints are rare in the calendar, not-
withstanding the splendid example of Michael,
" of celestial armies, prince," and there is at
present a shameless conspiracy on foot to
defraud even St. George of his hard-won glory,
and to melt him over in some modern crucible
into a peaceful Alexandrian bishop. An Arian
bishop, too, by way of deepening the scandal!
We shall hear next that Saint Denis was a
Calvinistic minister, and Saint Iago, whom
devout Spanish eyes have seen mounted in
the hottest of the fray, was a friendly well-
wisher of the Moors.

But why sigh over fighting saints, in a day
when even fighting sinners have scant measure
of praise? " Moral courage is everything.
Physical heroism is a small matter, often trivial enough," wrote that clever, emotional, sensitive German woman, Rahel Varnhagen, at
the very time when a little "physical heroism "
might have freed her conquered fatherland.
And this profession of faith has gone on increasing in popularity, until we have even a

lad like the young Laurence Oliphant, with hot blood surging in his veins, gravely recording his displeasure because a parson " with a Crimean medal on his surplice " preached a rousing battle sermon to the English soldiers who had no alternative but to fight. "My natural man," confesses Oliphant naïvely, " is intensely warlike, which is just as low a passion as avarice or any other," — a curious moral perspective, which needs no word of comment, and sufficiently explains much that was to follow. We are irresistibly reminded by such a verdict of Shelley's swelling lines —

> " War is the statesman's game, the priest's delight,
> The lawyer's jest, the hired assassin's trade ; "

lines which, to borrow a witticism of Mr. Oscar Wilde's, have " all the vitality of error," and will probably be quoted triumphantly by Peace Societies for many years to come.

In the mean time, there is a remarkable and very significant tendency to praise all war songs, war stories, and war literature generally, in proportion to the discomfort and horror they excite, in proportion to their inartistic and unjustifiable realism. I well remember, when I was a little girl, having a dismal

French tale by Erckmann-Chatrian, called "Le Conscrit," given me by a kindly disposed but mistaken friend, and the disgust with which I waded through those scenes of sordid bloodshed and misery, untouched by any fire of enthusiasm, any halo of romance. The very first description of Napoleon, — Napoleon, the idol of my youthful dreams, — as a fat, pale man, with a tuft of hair upon his forehead, filled me with loathing for all that was to follow. But I believe I finished the book, — it never occurred to me, in those innocent days, not to finish every book that I began, — and then I re-read in joyous haste all of Sir Walter Scott's fighting novels, "Waverley," "Old Mortality," "Ivanhoe," "Quentin Durward," and even "The Abbot," which has one good battle, to get the taste of that abominable story out of my mouth. Of late years, however, I have heard a great deal of French, Russian, and occasionally even English literature commended for the very qualities which aroused my childish indignation. No one has sung the praises of war more gallantly than Mr. Rudyard Kipling; yet those grim verses called "The Grave of the Hundred Dead" —

verses closely resembling the appalling specimens of truculency with which Mr. Ruskin
began and ended his brief poetical career
— have been singled out from their braver
brethren for especial praise, and offered as
" grim, naked, ugly truth " to those " who
would know more of the poet's picturesque
qualities."

But " grim, naked, ugly truth " can never be
made a picturesque quality, and it is not the
particular business of a battle poem to empha-
size the desirability of peace. We all know
the melancholy anticlimax of Campbell's
splendid song " Ye Mariners of England,"
when, to three admirable verses, the poet must
needs add a fourth, descriptive of the joys
of harmony, and of the eating and drinking
which shall replace the perils of the sea. I
count it a lasting injury, after having my
blood fired with these surging lines, —

> " Where Blake and mighty Nelson fell,
> Your manly hearts shall glow,
> As ye sweep through the deep,
> While the stormy winds do blow ;
> While the battle rages loud and long,
> And the stormy winds do blow," —

to be suddenly introduced to a scene of inglo-

rious junketing; and I am not surprised that
Campbell's peculiar inspiration, which was
born of war and of war only, failed him the
instant he deserted his theme. Such shocking
lines as

> " The meteor-flag of England
> Shall yet terrific burn,"

while quite in harmony with the poet's ordinary achievements, would have been simply
impossible in those first three verses of "Ye
Mariners," where he remains true to his one
artistic impulse. He strikes a different and a
finer note when, in " The Battle of the Baltic,"
he turns gravely away from feasting and jollity
to remember the brave men who have died for
England's glory : —

> " Let us think of them that sleep,
> Full many a fathom deep,
> By thy wild and stormy steep,
> Elsinore! "

To go back to Mr. Rudyard Kipling, however, from whom I have wandered far, he is
more in love with the " dear delights " of battle than with its dismal carnage, and he wins
an easy forgiveness for a few horrors by showing us much brave and hearty fighting. Who
can forget the little Gurkhas drawing a deep

breath of contentment when at last they see
the foe, and gaping expectantly at their officers, "as terriers grin ere the stone is cast
for them to fetch?" Who can forget the
joyous abandon with which Mulvaney the dis-
reputable and his "four an' twenty young
wans" fling themselves upon Lungtungpen?
It is a good and wholesome thing for a man
to be in sympathy with that primitive virtue,
courage, to recognize it promptly, and to do
honor to it under any flag. "Homer's heart
is with the brave of either side," observes
Mr. Lang; "with Glaucus and Sarpedon of
Lycia no less than with Achilles and Patroclus." Scott's heart is with Surrey and Dacre
no less than with Lennox and Argyle; with
the English hosts charging like whirlwinds to
the fray no less than with the Scottish soldiers
standing ringed and dauntless around their
king. Théodore de Banville, hot with shame
over fallen France, checks his bitterness to
write some tender verses to the memory of a
Prussian boy found dead on the field, with a
bullet-pierced volume of Pindar on his breast.
Dumas, that lover of all brave deeds, cries out
with noble enthusiasm that it was not enough

to kill the Highlanders at Waterloo, — " we
had to push them down! " and the reverse of
the medal has been shown us by Mr. Lang in
the letter of an English officer, who writes
home that he would have given the rest of his
life to have served with the French cavalry on
that awful day. Sir Francis Doyle delights,
like an honest and stout-hearted Briton, to pay
an equal tribute of praise, in rather questionable verse, to the private of the Buffs,

> " Poor, reckless, rude, low-born, untaught,
> Bewildered and alone, "

who died for England's honor in a far-off
land; and to the Indian prince, Mehrab
Khan, who, brought to bay, swore proudly
that he would perish,

> " to the last the lord
> Of all that man can call his own, "

and fell beneath the English bayonets at the
door of his zenana. This is the spirit by
which brave men know one another the world
over, and which, lying back of all healthy
national prejudices, unites in a human brother-
hood those whom the nearness of death has
taught to start at no shadows.

" Oh, east is east, and west is west, and never the two shall
  meet
Till earth and sky stand presently at God's great Judgment
  Seat.
But there is neither east nor west, border nor breed nor
  birth,
When two strong men stand face to face, though they come
  from the ends of the earth."

Here is Mr. Kipling at his best, and here,
too, is a link somewhat simpler and readier to
hand than that much-desired bond of cultiva-
tion which Mr. Oscar Wilde assures us will
one day knit the world together. The time
when Germany will no longer hate France,
"because the prose of France is perfect,"
seems still as far-off as it is fair; the day when
"intellectual criticism will bind Europe together" dawns only in the dreamland of
desire. Mr. Wilde makes himself merry at
the expense of "Peace Societies, so dear to
the sentimentalists, and proposals for unarmed
International Arbitration, so popular among
those who have never read history;" but criticism, the mediator of the future, "will anni-
hilate race prejudices by insisting upon the
unity of the human mind in the variety of its
forms. If we are tempted to make war upon

another nation, we shall remember that we are
seeking to destroy an element of our own culture, and possibly its most important element."
This restraining impulse will allow us to fight
only red Indians, and Feejeeans, and Bush-
men, from whom no grace of culture is to be
gleaned; and it may prove a strong induce-
ment to some disturbed countries, like Ireland
and Russia, to advance a little further along
the paths of sweetness and light. Meanwhile,
the world, which rolls so easily in old and
well-worn ways, will probably remember that
"power is measured by resistance," and will
go on arguing stolidly in platoons.

"All healthy men like fighting and like the
sense of danger; all brave women like to hear
of their fighting and of their facing danger,"
says Mr. Ruskin, who has taken upon himself
the defense of war in his own irresistibly un-
convincing manner. Others indeed have delighted in it from a purely artistic standpoint,
or as a powerful stimulus to fancy. Mr.
Saintsbury exults more than most critics in
battle poems, and in those "half-inarticulate
songs that set the blood coursing." Sir Francis Doyle, whose simple manly soul never

wearied of such themes, had no ambition to outgrow the first hearty sympathies of his boyhood. "I knew the battle in 'Marmion' by heart almost before I could read," he writes in his "Reminiscences;" "and I cannot raze out — I do not wish to raze out — of my soul all that filled and colored it in years gone by." Mr. Froude, who is as easily seduced by the picturesqueness of a sea fight as was Canon Kingsley, appears to believe in all seriousness that the British privateers who went plundering in the Spanish main were inspired by a pure love for England, and a zeal for the Protestant faith. He can say truly with the little boy of adventurous humor, —

> "There is something that suits my mind to a T
> In the thought of a reg'lar Pirate King."

Mr. Lang's love of all warlike literature is too well known to need comment. As a child, he confesses he pored over "the fightingest parts of the Bible," when Sunday deprived him of less hallowed reading. As a boy, he devoted to Sir Walter Scott the precious hours which were presumably sacred to the shrine of Latin grammar. As a man, he lures us with glowing words from the consideration of politi-

cal problems, or of our own complicated spiritual machinery, to follow the fortunes of the
brave, fierce men who fought in the lonely
north, or of the heroes who went forth in
gilded armor "to win glory or to give it" before the walls of Troy. In these days, when
many people find it easier to read " The Ring
and the Book" than the Iliad, Mr. Lang makes
a strong plea in behalf of that literature which
has come down to us out of the past to stand
forevermore unrivaled and alone, stirring the
hearts of all generations until human nature
shall be warped from simple and natural lines.
" With the Bible and Shakespeare," he says,
" the Homeric poems are the best training for
life. There is no good quality that they lack;
manliness, courage, reverence for old age and
for the hospitable hearth, justice, piety, pity,
a brave attitude towards life and death, are all
conspicuous in Homer." It might be well,
perhaps, to add to this long list one more incomparable virtue, an instinctive and illogical
delight in living. Amid shipwrecks and battles, amid long wanderings and hurtling spears,
amid sharp dangers and sorrows bitter to bear,
Homer teaches us, and teaches us in right joy-

ful fashion, the beauty and value of an existence which we profess nowadays to find a little burdensome on our hands.

All these things have the lovers of war said to us, and in all these ways have they striven to fire our hearts. But Mr. Rúskin is not content to regard any matter from a purely artistic standpoint, or to judge it on natural and congenital lines ; he must indorse it ethically or condemn. Accordingly, it is not enough for him, as it would be for any other man, to claim that "no great art ever yet rose on earth but among a nation of soldiers." He feels it necessary to ask himself some searching and embarrassing questions about fighting "for its own sake," and as "a grand pastime," — questions which he naturally finds it extremely difficult to answer. It is not enough for him to say, with equal truth and justice, that if "brave death in a red coat " be no better than "brave life in a black one," it is at least every bit as good. He must needs wax serious, and commit himself to this strong and doubtful statement : —

" Assume the knight merely to have ridden out occasionally to fight his neighbor for exer-

cise; assume him even a soldier of fortune,
and to have gained his bread and filled his
purse at the sword's point. Still I feel as if
it were, somehow, grander and worthier in him
to have made his bread by sword play than
any other play. I had rather he had made
it by thrusting than by batting, — much more
than by betting; much rather that he should
ride war horses than back race horses; and —
I say it sternly and deliberately — much
rather would I have him slay his neighbor
than cheat him."

Perhaps, in deciding a point as delicate as
this, it would not be altogether amiss to con-
sult the subject acted upon; in other words,
the neighbor, who, whatever may be his prejudice against dishonest handling, might probably prefer it to the last irredeemable disaster.
In this commercial age we get tolerably accustomed to being cheated — like the skinned
eel, we are used to it, — but there is an old
rhyme which tells us plainly that a broken
neck is beyond all help of healing.

No, it is best, when we treat a theme as
many-sided as war, to abandon modern in-
quisitorial methods, and confine ourselves to

that good old-fashioned simplicity which was content to take short obvious views of life. It is best to leave ethics alone, and ride as lightly as we may. The finest poems of battle and of camp have been written in this unincumbered spirit, as, for example, that lovely little snatch of song from " Rokeby : " —

> " A weary lot is thine, fair maid,
>   A weary lot is thine !
> To pull the thorn thy brow to braid,
>   And press the rue for wine.
> A lightsome eye, a soldier's mien,
>   A feather of the blue,
> A doublet of the Lincoln green, —
>   No more of me you knew,
>   My love !
>   No more of me you knew."

And this other, far less familiar, which I quote from Lockhart's Spanish Ballads, and which is fitly called " The Wandering Knight's Song : " —

> " My ornaments are arms,
>   My pastime is in war,
> My bed is cold upon the wold,
>   My lamp yon star.
>
> " My journeyings are long,
>   My slumbers short and broken ;
> From hill to hill I wander still,
>   Kissing thy token.

"I ride from land to land,
　I sail from sea to sea;
Some day more kind I fate may find,
　Some night, kiss thee."

Now, apart from the charming felicity of these lines, we cannot but be struck with their singleness of conception and purpose. "The Wandering Knight" is well-nigh as disincumbered of mental as of material luggage. He rides as free from our tangled perplexity of introspection as from our irksome contrivances for comfort. It is not that he is precisely guileless or ignorant. One does not journey far over the world without learning the world's ways, and the ways of the men who dwell upon her. But the knowledge of things looked at from the outside is never the knowledge that wears one's soul away, and the traveling companion that Lord Byron found so *ennuyant*,

"The blight of life — the demon Thought,"

forms no part of the "Wandering Knight's" equipment. As I read this little fugitive song which has drifted down into an alien age, I feel an envious liking for those days when the tumult of existence made its triumph, when action fanned the embers of joy, and when

people were too busy with each hour of life, as
it came, to question the usefulness or desirability of the whole.

There is one more point to consider.   Mr.
Saintsbury appears to think it strange that
battles, when they occur, and especially when
they chance to be victories, should not imme-
diately inspire good war songs.   But this is
seldom or never the case, " The Charge of the
Light Brigade " being an honorable exception
to the rule.   Drayton's heroic ballad was written nearly two hundred years after the battle
of Agincourt; Flodden is a tale of defeat;
and Campbell, whose songs are so intoxicat-
ingly warlike, belonged, I am sorry to say, to
the " Peace at all price" party.   The fact is
that a battle fought five hundred years ago is
just as inspiring to the poet as a battle fought
yesterday; and a brave deed, the memory of
which comes down to us through centuries,
stirs our hearts as profoundly as though we
witnessed it in our own time.   Sarpedon, leap-
ing lightly from his chariot to dare an unequal combat; the wounded knight, Schön-
burg, dragging himself painfully from amid
the dead and dying to offer his silver shield to

his defenseless emperor ; the twenty kinsmen
of the noble family of Trauttmansdorf who
fell, under Frederick of Austria, in the single
battle of Mühldorf; the English lad, young
Anstruther, who carried the queen's colors of
the Royal Welsh at the storming of Sebasto-
pol, and who, swift-footed as a schoolboy, was
the first to gain the great redoubt, and stood
there one happy moment, holding his flagstaff
and breathing hard, before he was shot dead,
— these are the pictures whose value distance
can never lessen, and whose colors time can
never dim. These are the deeds that belong
to all ages and to all nations, a heritage for
every man who walks this troubled earth.
" All this the gods have fashioned, and have
woven the skein of death for men, that there
might be a song in the ears even of the folk
of after time."

LEISURE.

" Zounds ! how has he the leisure to be sick ? "

A VISITOR strolling through the noble woods of Ferney complimented Voltaire on the splendid growth of his trees. "Ay," replied the great wit, half in scorn and half, perhaps, in envy, " they have nothing else to do ; " and walked on, deigning no further word of approbation.

Has it been more than a hundred years since this distinctly modern sentiment was uttered, — more than a hundred years since the spreading chestnut boughs bent kindly over the lean, strenuous, caustic, disappointed man of genius who always had so much to do, and who found in the doing of it a mingled bliss and bitterness that scorched him like fever pain ? How is it that, while Dr. Johnson's sledge-hammer repartees sound like the sonorous echoes of a past age, Voltaire's remarks always appear to have been

spoken the day before yesterday? They are
the kind of witticisms which we do not say
for ourselves, simply because we are not witty ;
but they illustrate with biting accuracy the
spirit of restlessness, of disquiet, of intellectual vanity and keen contention which is the
brand of our vehement and over-zealous generation.

" The Gospel of Work " — that is the phrase
woven insistently into every homily, every
appeal made to the conscience or the intelligence of a people who are now straining their
youthful energy to its utmost speed. " Blessed
be Drudgery ! " — that is the text deliberately
chosen for a discourse which has enjoyed such
amazing popularity that sixty thousand printed
copies have been found all inadequate to supply the ravenous demand. Readers of Dickens — if any one has the time to read Dickens
nowadays — may remember Miss Monflather's
inspired amendment of that familiar poem
concerning the Busy Bee : —

> " In work, work, work. In work alway,
> Let my first years be past."

And when our first years *are* past, the same
programme is considered adequate and satis-

factory to the end. "A whole lifetime of horrid industry," — to quote Mr. Bagehot's uninspired words, — this is the prize dangled alluringly before our tired eyes; and if we are disposed to look askance upon the booty, then vanity is subtly pricked to give zest to faltering resolution. "Our virtues would be proud if our faults whipped them not;" they would be laggards in the field if our faults did not sometimes spur them to action. It is the pæan of self-glorification that wells up perpetually from press and pulpit, from public orators, and from what is courteously called literature, that keeps our courage screwed to the sticking place, and veils the occasional bareness of the result with a charitable vesture of self-delusion.

Work is good. No one seriously doubts this truth. Adam may have doubted it when he first took spade in hand, and Eve when she scoured her first pots and kettles; but in the course of a few thousand years we have learned to know and value this honest, troublesome, faithful, and extremely exacting friend. But work is not the only good thing in the world; it is not a fetich to be adored :

neither is it to be judged, like a sum in addition, by its outward and immediate results. The god of labor does not abide exclusively in the rolling-mill, the law courts, or the cornfield. He has a twin sister whose name is leisure, and in her society he lingers now and then to the lasting gain of both.

Sainte-Beuve, writing of Mme. de Sévigné and her time, says that we, "with our habits of positive occupation, can scarcely form a just conception of that life. of leisure and chit-chat." "Conversations were infinite," admits Mme. de Sévigné herself, recalling the long summer afternoons when she and her guests walked in the charming woods of Les Rochers until the shadows of twilight fell. The whole duty of life seemed to be concentrated in the pleasant task of entertaining your friends when they were with you, or writing them admirable letters when they were absent. Occasionally there came, even to this tranquil and finely poised French woman, a haunting consciousness that there might be other and harder work for human hands to do. "Nothing is accomplished day by day," she writes, doubtfully; "and life is

made up of days, and we grow old and die."
This troubled her a little, when she was all
the while doing work that was to last for
generations, work that was to give pleasure
to men and women whose great-grandfathers
were then unborn. Not that we have the
time now to read Mme. de Sévigné! Why,
there are big volumes of these delightful
letters, and who can afford to read big volumes of anything, merely for the sake of the
enjoyment to be extracted therefrom? It was
all very well for Sainte-Beuve to say " Lisons
tout Mme. de Sévigné," when the question
arose how should some long idle days in a
country-house be profitably employed. It was
all very well for Sainte-Beuve to plead, with
touching confidence in the intellectual pastimes of his contemporaries, " Let us treat
Mme. de Sévigné as we treat Clarissa Harlowe, when we have a fortnight of leisure
and rainy weather in the country." A fortnight of leisure and rainy weather in the
country! The words would be antiquated
even for Dr. Johnson. Rain may fall or rain
may cease, but leisure comes not so lightly
to our calling. Nay, Sainte-Beuve's wistful

amazement at the polished and cultivated inactivity which alone could produce such a correspondence as Mme. de Sévigné's is not greater than our wistful amazement at the critic's conception of possible idleness in bad weather. In one respect at least we follow his good counsel. We do treat Mme. de Sévigné precisely as we treat Clarissa Harlowe; that is, we leave them both severely alone, as being utterly beyond the reach of what we are pleased to call our time.

And what of the leisure of Montaigne, who, taking his life in his two hands, disposed of it as he thought fit, with no restless self-accusations on the score of indolence. In the world and of the world, yet always able to meet and greet the happy solitude of Gascony; toiling with no thought of toil, but rather " to entertaine my spirit as it best pleased," this man wrought out of time a coin which passes current over the reading world. And what of Horace, who enjoyed an industrious idleness, the bare description of which sets our hearts aching with desire ! " The picture which Horace draws of himself in his country home," says an envious English critic,

" affords us a delightful glimpse of such literary leisure as is only possible in the golden days of good Haroun-Al-Raschid. Horace goes to bed and gets up when he likes; there is no one to drag him down to the law courts the first thing in the morning, to remind him of an important engagement with his brother scribes, to solicit his interest with Mæcenas, or to tease him about public affairs and the latest news from abroad. He can bury himself in his Greek authors, or ramble through the woody glens which lie at the foot of Mount Ustica, without a thought of business or a feeling that he ought to be otherwise engaged." "Swim smoothly in the stream of thy nature, and live but one man," counsels Sir Thomas Browne; and it may be this gentle current will bear us as bravely through life as if we buffeted our strength away in the restless ocean of endeavor.

Leisure has a value of its own. It is not a mere handmaid of labor; it is something we should know how to cultivate, to use, and to enjoy. It has a distinct and honorable place wherever nations are released from the pressure of their first rude needs, their first homely

toil, and rise to happier levels of grace and
intellectual repose. "Civilization, in its final
outcome," says the keen young author of
" The Chevalier of Pensieri-Vani," " is heavily
in the debt of leisure ; and the success of any
society worth considering is to be estimated
largely by the use to which its *fortunati* put
their spare moments." Here is a sentiment
so relentlessly true that nobody wants to believe it. We prefer uttering agreeable plati-
tudes concerning the blessedness of drudgery
and the iniquity of eating bread earned by
another's hands. Yet the creation of an artistic and intellectual atmosphere in which
workers can work, the expansion of a noble
sympathy with all that is finest and most
beautiful, the jealous guardianship of whatever makes the glory and distinction of a
nation ; this is achievement enough for the
fortunati of any land, and this is the debt
they owe. It can hardly be denied that the
lack of scholarship — of classical scholarship
especially — at our universities is due pri-
marily to the labor-worship which is the prevalent superstition of our day, and which, like
all superstitions, has gradually degraded its

god into an idol, and lost sight of the higher powers and attributes beyond. The student who is pleased to think a knowledge of German "more useful" than a knowledge of Greek; the parent who deliberately declares that his boys have "no time to waste" over Homer; the man who closes the doors of his mind to everything that does not bear directly on mathematics, or chemistry, or engineering, or whatever he calls "work;" all these plead in excuse the exigencies of life, the absolute and imperative necessity of labor.

It would appear, then, that we have no *fortunati*, that we are not yet rich enough to afford the greatest of all luxuries — leisure to cultivate and enjoy " the best that has been known and thought in the world." This is a pity, because there seems to be money in plenty for so many less valuable things. The yearly taxes of the United States sound to innocent ears like the fabled wealth of the Orient; the yearly expenditures of the people are on no rigid scale; yet we are too poor to harbor the priceless literature of the past because it is not a paying investment, because it will not put bread in our mouths nor clothes on our shivering nakedness. " Poverty is a most odious calling," sighed Burton many years ago, and we have good cause to echo his lament. Until we are able to believe, with that enthusiastic Greek scholar, Mr. Butcher, that " intellectual training is an end in itself, and not a mere preparation for a trade or a profession ; " until we begin to understand that there is a leisure which does not mean an easy sauntering through life, but a special form of activity, employing all our faculties, and training us to the adequate reception of whatever is most valuable in literature and art ; until we learn to estimate the fruits of self-culture at their proper worth, we are still far from reaping the harvest of three centuries of toil and struggle ; we are still as remote as ever from the serenity of intellectual accomplishment.

There is a strange pleasure in work wedded to leisure, in work which has grown beautiful because its rude necessities are softened and humanized by sentiment and the subtle grace of association. A little paragraph from the journal of Eugénie de Guérin illustrates with charming simplicity the gilding of common toil by the delicate touch of a cultivated and sympathetic intelligence : —

" A day spent in spreading out a large wash leaves little to say, and yet it is rather pretty, too, to lay the white linen on the grass, or to see it float on lines. One may fancy one's self Homer's Nausicaa, or one of those Biblical princesses who washed their brothers' tunics. We have a basin at Moulinasse that you have never seen, sufficiently large, and full to the brim of water. It embellishes the hollow, and attracts the birds who like a cool place to sing in."

In the same spirit, Maurice de Guérin confesses frankly the pleasure he takes in gathering fagots for the winter fire, " that little task of the woodcutter which brings us close to nature," and which was also a favorite occupation of M. de Lamennais. The fagot gathering, indeed, can hardly be said to have assumed the proportions of real toil; it was rather a pastime where play was thinly disguised by a pretty semblance of drudgery. " Idleness," admits de Guérin, " *but idleness full of thought, and alive to every impression.*" Eugénie's labors, however, had other aspects and bore different fruit. There is nothing intrinsically charming in stitching seams, hanging out clothes, or scorching one's fingers over a kitchen fire; yet every page in the journal of this nobly born French girl reveals to us the nearness of work, work made sacred by the prompt fulfillment of visible duties, and — what is more rare — made beautiful by that distinction of mind which was the result of alternating hours of finely cultivated leisure. A very ordinary and estimable young woman might have spread her wash upon the grass with honest pride at the white ness of her linen; but it needed the solitude of Le Cayla, the few books, well read and well worth reading, the life of patriarchal simplicity, and the habit of sustained and delicate thought, to awaken in the worker's mind the graceful association of ideas, — the pretty picture of Nausicaa and her maidens cleansing their finely woven webs in the cool, rippling tide.

For it is self-culture that warms the chilly earth wherein no good seed can mature; it is self-culture that distinguishes between the work which has inherent and lasting value and the work which represents conscientious activity and no more. And for the training

of one's self, leisure is requisite ; leisure and
that rare modesty which turns a man's
thoughts back to his own shortcomings and
requirements, and extinguishes in him the
burning desire to enlighten his fellow-beings.
"We might make ourselves spiritual by de-
taching ourselves from action, and become
perfect by the rejection of energy," says Mr.
Oscar Wilde, who delights in scandalizing his
patient readers, and who lapses unconsciously
into something resembling animation over the
wrongs inflicted by the solemn preceptors of
mankind. The notion that it is worth while
to learn a thing only if you intend to impart
it to others is widespread and exceedingly
popular. I have myself heard an excellent
and anxious aunt say to her young niece,
then working hard at college, " But, my dear,
why do you give so much of your time to
Greek? You don't expect to teach it, do
you ?" — as if there were no other use to
be gained, no other pleasure to be won from
that noble language, in which lies hidden
the hoarded treasure of centuries. To study
Greek in order to read and enjoy it, and
thereby make life better worth the living,

is a possibility that seldom enters the practical modern mind.

Yet this restless desire to give out information, like alms, is at best a questionable bounty; this determination to share one's wisdom with one's unwilling fellow-creatures is a noble impulse provocative of general discontent. When Southey, writing to James Murray about a dialogue which he proposes to publish in the " Quarterly," says, with characteristic complacency: " I have very little doubt that it will excite considerable attention, and lead many persons into a wholesome train of thought, " we feel at once how absolutely familiar is the sentiment, and how absolutely hopeless is literature approached in this spirit. The same principle, working under different conditions to-day, entangles us in a network of lectures, which have become the chosen field for every educational novelty, and the diversion of the mentally unemployed.

Charles Lamb has recorded distinctly his veneration for the old-fashioned schoolmaster who taught his Greek and Latin in leisurely fashion day after day, with no thought wasted upon more superficial or practical acquirements,

and who "came to his task as to a sport." He
has made equally plain his aversion for the new-
fangled pedagogue — new in his time, at least
— who could not "relish a beggar or a gypsy"
without seeking to collect or to impart some
statistical information on the subject.   A gentleman of this calibre, his fellow - traveler in
a coach, once asked him if he had ever made
"any calculation as to the value of the rental
of all the retail shops in London?" and the
magnitude of the question so overwhelmed
Lamb that he could not even stammer out a
confession of his ignorance.   "To go preach
to the first passer-by, to become tutor to the
ignorance of the first thing I meet, is a task
I abhor," observes Montaigne, who must certainly have been the most acceptable companion of his day.

Dr. Johnson, too, had scant sympathy with
insistent and arrogant industry.   He could
work hard enough when circumstances demanded it; but he "always felt an inclination
to do nothing," and not infrequently gratified
his desires.   "No man, sir, is obliged to do as
much as he can.   A man should have part of
his life to himself," was the good doctor's

soundly heterodox view, advanced upon many occasions. He hated to hear people boast of their assiduity, and nipped such vain pretensions in the bud with frosty scorn. When he and Boswell journeyed together in the Harwich stage-coach, a "fat, elderly gentle-woman," who had been talking freely of her own affairs, wound up by saying that she never permitted any of her children to be for a moment idle. "I wish, madam," said Dr. Johnson testily, "that you would educate me too, for I have been an idle fellow all my life." "I am sure, sir," protested the woman with dismayed politeness, "you have not been idle." "Madam," was the retort, "it is true! And that gentleman there" — pointing to poor young Boswell — "has been idle also. He was idle in Edinburgh. His father sent him to Glasgow, where he continued to be idle. He came to London, where he has been very idle. And now he is going to Utrecht, where he will be as idle as ever."

That there was a background of truth in these spirited assertions we have every reason to be grateful. Dr. Johnson's value to-day does not depend on the number of essays, or

reviews, or dedications he wrote in a year, —
some years he wrote nothing, — but on his own
sturdy and splendid personality; "the real
primate, the soul's teacher of all England,"
says Carlyle ; a great embodiment of uncom-
promising goodness and sense.   Every generation needs such a man, not to compile dictionaries, but to preserve the balance of sanity,
and few generations are blest enough to possess
him.   As for Boswell, he might have toiled in
the law courts until he was gray without ben-
efiting or amusing anybody.   It was in the
nights he spent drinking port wine at the
Mitre, and in the days he spent trotting, like
a terrier, at his master's heels, that the seed
was sown which was to give the world a mas-
terpiece of literature, the most delightful bi-
ography that has ever enriched mankind.   It
is to leisure that we owe the " Life of Johnson,"
and a heavy debt we must, in all integrity,
acknowledge it to be.

Mr. Shortreed said truly of Sir Walter
Scott that he was "making himself in the
busy, idle pleasures of his youth; " in those
long rambles by hill and dale, those whimsical
adventures in farmhouses, those merry, pur-

poseless journeys in which the eager lad tasted
the flavor of life. At home such unauthor-
ized amusements were regarded with emphatic
disapprobation. "I greatly doubt, sir," said
his father to him one day, "that you were
born for nae better than a gangrel scrape-gut!"
and one half pities the grave clerk to the Sig-
net, whose own life had been so decorously
dull, and who regarded with affectionate solicitude his lovable and incomprehensible son.
In later years Sir Walter recognized keenly
that his wasted school hours entailed on him a
lasting loss, a loss he was determined his sons
should never know. It is to be forever re-
gretted that "the most Homeric of modern
men could not read Homer." But every day
he stole from the town to give to the country,
every hour he stole from law to give to literature, every minute he stole from work to
give to pleasure, counted in the end as gain.
It is in his pleasures that a man really lives,
it is from his leisure that he constructs the true
fabric of self. Perhaps Charles Lamb's fellow-
clerks thought that because his days were
spent at a desk in the East India House, his
life was spent there too. His life was far

remote from that routine of labor ; built up of golden moments of respite, enriched with joys, chastened by sorrows, vivified by impulses that had no filiation with his daily toil. " For the time that a man may call his own," he writes to Wordsworth, " that is his life." The Lamb who worked in the India House, and who had "no skill in figures," has passed away, and is to-day but a shadow and a name. The Lamb of the " Essays " and the " Letters " lives for us now, and adds each year his generous share to the innocent gayety of the world. This is the Lamb who said, " Riches are chiefly good because they give us time," and who sighed for a little son that he might christen him Nothing-to-do, and permit him to do nothing.

WORDS.

"Do you read the dictionary?" asked M. Théophile Gautier of a young and ardent disciple who had come to him for counsel. "It is the most fruitful and interesting of books. Words have an individual and a relative value. They should be chosen before being placed in position. This word is a mere pebble; that a fine pearl or an amethyst. In art the handicraft is everything, and the absolute distinction of the artist lies, not so much in his capacity to feel nature, as in his power to render it."

We are always pleased to have a wholesome truth presented to us with such genial vivacity, so that we may feel ourselves less edified than diverted, and learn our lesson without the mortifying consciousness of ignorance. He is a wise preceptor who conceals from us his awful rod of office, and grafts his knowledge dexterously upon our self-esteem.

" Men must be taught as if you taught them not,
  And things unknown proposed as things forgot."

An appreciation of words is so rare that everybody naturally thinks he possesses it, and this
universal sentiment results in the misuse of
a material whose beauty enriches the loving
student beyond the dreams of avarice. Mu-
sicians know the value of chords; painters
know the value of colors; writers are often so
blind to the value of words that they are content with a bare expression of their thoughts,
disdaining the "labor of the file," and confi-
dent that the phrase first seized is for them
the phrase of inspiration. They exaggerate
the importance of what they have to say, —
lacking which we should be none the poorer, —
and underrate the importance of saying it in
such fashion that we may welcome its very
moderate significance. It is in the habitual
and summary recognition of the laws of language that scholarship delights, says Mr.
Pater; and while the impatient thinker, eager
only to impart his views, regards these laws
as a restriction, the true artist finds in them
an opportunity, and rejoices, as Goethe re-
joiced, to work within conditions and limits.

For every sentence that may be penned or
spoken the right words exist. They lie concealed in the inexhaustible wealth of a vocabulary enriched by centuries of noble thought
and delicate manipulation. He who does not
find them and fit 'them into place, who accepts the first term which presents itself rather
than search for the expression which accurately and beautifully embodies his meaning,
aspires to mediocrity, and is content with fail-
ure. The exquisite adjustment of a word to
its significance, which was the instrument of
Flaubert's daily martyrdom and daily triumph ;
the generous sympathy of a word with its
surroundings, which was the secret wrung by
Sir Thomas Browne from the mysteries of
language, — these are the twin perfections
which constitute style, and substantiate genius.
Cardinal Newman also possesses in an extraordinary degree Flaubert's art of fitting his
words to the exact thoughts they are designed
to convey. Such a brief sentence as " Ten
thousand difficulties do not make one doubt "
reveals with pregnant simplicity the mental
attitude of the writer. Sir Thomas Browne,
working under fewer restraints, and without

the severity of intellectual discipline, harmo-
nizes each musical syllable into a prose of
leisurely sweetness and sonorous strength.
" Court not felicity too far, and weary not the
favorable hand of fortune." " Man is a noble
animal, splendid in ashes, and pompous in the
grave." " The race of delight is short, and
pleasures have mutable faces." Such sentences,
woven with curious skill from the rich fabric
of seventeenth - century English, defy the
wreckage of time. In them a gentle dignity
of thought finds its appropriate expression,
and the restfulness of an unvexed mind
breathes its quiet beauty into each cadenced
line. Here are no " boisterous metaphors,"
such as Dryden scorned, to give undue emphasis at every turn, and amaze the careless
reader with the cheap delights of turbulence.
Here is no trace of that " full habit of
speech," hateful to Mr. Arnold's soul, and
which, in the years to come, was to be the gift
of journalism to literature.

The felicitous choice of words, which with
most writers is the result of severe study and
unswerving vigilance, seems with a favored
few — who should be envied and not imitated

— to be the genuine fruit of inspiration, as though caprice itself could not lead them far astray. Shelley's letters and prose papers teem with sentences in which the beautiful . words are sufficient satisfaction in themselves, and of more value than the conclusions they reveal. They have a haunting sweetness, a pure perfection, which makes the act of reading them a sustained and dulcet pleasure. Sometimes this effect is produced by a few simple terms reiterated into lingering music. " We are born, and our birth is unremembered, and our infancy remembered but in fragments; we live on, and in living we lose the apprehension of life." Sometimes a clearer note is struck with the sure and delicate touch which is the excellence of art. " For the mind in creation is as a fading coal, which some invisible influence, like an inconstant wind, awakens to transitory brightness." The substitution of the word " glow " for " brightness " would, I think, make this sentence extremely beautiful. If it lacks the fullness and melody of those incomparable passages in which Burke, the great master of words, rivets our admiration forever, it has the same peculiar and lasting

hold upon our imaginations and our memories. Once read, we can no more forget its
charm than we can forget "that chastity of
honor which felt a stain like a wound," or
the mournful cadence of regret over virtues
deemed superfluous in an age of strictly icon-
oclastic progress. "Never more shall we behold that generous loyalty to rank and sex,
that proud submission, that dignified obedience, that subordination of the heart which
kept alive, even in servitude itself, the spirit
of an exalted freedom." It is the fashion
at present to subtly depreciate Burke's power
by some patronizing allusion to the "grand
style," — a phrase which, except when applied
to Milton, appears to hold in solution an un-
defined and undefinable reproach. But until
we can produce something better, or something as good, those "long savorsome Latin
words," checked and vivified by "racy Saxon
monosyllables," must still represent an excellence which it is easier to belittle than to
emulate.

It is strange that our chilling disapprobation of what we are prone to call "fine writing" melts into genial applause over the

freakish perversity so dear to modern unrest.
We look askance upon such an old-time master of his craft as the Opium-Eater, and require to be told by a clear-headed, unenthusi-
astic critic like Mr. George Saintsbury that
the balanced harmony of De Quincey's style
is obtained often by the use of extremely
simple words, couched in the clearest imagi-
nable form. Place by the side of Mr. Pater's
picture of Monna Lisa — too well known to
need quotation — De Quincey's equally famous
description of Our Lady of Darkness. Both
passages are as beautiful as words can make
them, but the gift of simplicity is in the
hands of the older writer. Or take the single
sentence which describes for us the mystery of
Our Lady of Sighs: "And her eyes, if they
were ever seen, would be neither sweet nor
subtle; no man could read their story; they
would be found filled with perishing dreams,
and with wrecks of forgotten delirium."
Here, as Mr. Saintsbury justly points out, are
no needless adjectives, no unusual or extrava-
gant words. The sense is adequate to the
sound, and the sound is only what is required
as accompaniment to the sense. We are not

perplexed and startled, as when Browning introduces us to

"the Tyrrhene whelk's pearl-sheeted lip,"

or to a woman's

"morbid, olive, faultless shoulder-blades."

We are not irritated and confused, as when Carlyle — whose misdeeds, like those of Browning, are matters of pure volition — is pleased, for our sharper discipline, to write "like a comet inscribing with its tail." No man uses words more admirably, or abuses them more shamefully, than Carlyle. That he should delight in seeing his pages studded all over with such spikes as "mammonism," "flunkeyhood," "nonentity," and "simulacrum," that he should repeat them again and again with unwearying self-content, is an enigma that defies solution, save on the simple presumption that they are designed, like other instruments of torture, to test the fortitude of the sufferer. It is best to scramble over them as bravely as we can, and forget our scars in the enjoyment of those vivid and matchless pictures in which each word plays its part, and supplies its share of outline and emphasis to the scene. The art that can dictate such a brief bit of description as " little red-colored pulpy infants " is the art of a Dutch master who, on five inches of canvas, depicts for us with subdued vehemence the absolute realities of life.

" All freaks," remarks Mr. Arnold, "tend to impair the beauty and power of language ; " yet so prone are we to confuse the bizarre with the picturesque that at present a great deal of English literature resembles a linguistic museum, where every type of monstrosity is cheerfully exhibited and admired. Writers of splendid capacity, of undeniable originality and force, are not ashamed to add their curios to the group, either from sheer impatience of restraint, or, as I sometimes think, from a grim and perverted sense of humor, which is enlivened by noting how far they can venture beyond bounds. When Mr. George Meredith is pleased to tell us that one of his characters "neighed a laugh," that another " tolled her naughty head," that a third " stamped ; her aspect spat," and that a fourth was discovered " pluming a smile upon his succulent mouth," we cannot smother a dawning suspicion that

he is diverting himself at our expense, and
pluming a smile of his own, more sapless than
succulent, over the naïve simplicity of the
public. Perhaps it is a yearning after subtlety
rather than a spirit of uncurbed humor which
prompts Vernon Lee to describe for us Carlo's
" dark Renaissance face perplexed with an in-
cipient laugh; " but really a very interesting
and improving little paper might be written
on the extraordinary laughs and smiles which
cheer the somewhat saturnine pages of modern
analytic fiction. " Correctness, that humble
merit of prose," has been snubbed into a recognition of her insignificance. She is as
tame as a woman with only one head and
two arms amid her more striking and richly
endowed sisters in the museum.

" A language long employed by a delicate
and critical society," says Mr. Walter Bagehot, " is a treasure of dexterous felicities ; "
and to awaken the literary conscience to its
forgotten duty of guarding this treasure is the
avowed vocation of Mr. Pater, and of another
stylist, less understood and less appreciated,
Mr. Oscar Wilde. Their labors are scantily
rewarded in an age which has but little in-

stinct for form, and which habitually allows itself the utmost license of phraseology. That " unblessed freedom from restraint," which to the clear-eyed Greeks appeared diametrically opposed to a wise and well-ordered liberty, and which finds its amplest expression in the poems of Walt Whitman, has dazzled us only to betray. The emancipation of the savage is sufficiently comprehensive, but his privileges are not always as valuable as they may at first sight appear. Mr. Brownell, in his admirable volume " French Traits," unhesitatingly defines Whitman's slang as " the riotous medium of the under-languaged ; " and the reproach is not too harsh nor too severe. Even Mr. G. C. Macaulay, one of the most acute and enthusiastic of his English critics, admits sadly that it is " gutter slang," equally purposeless and indefensible. That a man who held within himself the elements of greatness should have deliberately lessened the force of his life's work by a willful misuse of his material is one of those bitter and irremediable errors which sanity forever deplores. We are inevitably repelled by the employment of trivial or vulgar words in serious

poetry, and they become doubly offensive
when brought into relation with the beauty
and majesty of nature. It is neither pleasant
nor profitable to hear the sun's rays described
as

"scooting obliquely high and low."

It is still less satisfactory to have the universe
addressed in this convivial and burlesque fashion : —

"Earth, you seem to look for something at my hands;
Say, old Topknot, what do you want ? "

There is a kind of humorousness which a true
sense of humor would render impossible;
there is a species of originality from which the
artist shrinks aghast; and worse than mere
vulgarity is the constant employment of words
indecorous in themselves, and irreverent in
their application, — the smirching of clean
and noble things with adjectives grossly un-
fitted for such use, and repellent to all the
canons of good taste. This is not the " gentle
pressure " which Sophocles put upon common
words to wring from them a fresh significance;
it is a deliberate abuse of terms, and betrays
a lack of that fine quality of self-repression
which embraces the power of selection, and is

the best characteristic of literary morality. " Oh, for the style of honest men ! " sighs Sainte-Beuve, sick of such unreserved dis- closures ; " of men who have revered every- thing worthy of respect, whose innate feelings have ever been governed by the principles of good taste. Oh, for the polished, pure, and moderate writers ! "

There is a pitiless French maxim, less pop- ular with English and Americans than with our Gallic neighbors, — " Le secret d'ennuyer est de tout dire." Mr. Pater indeed expresses the same thought in ampler English fashion (which but emphasizes the superiority of the French) when he says, " For in truth all art does but consist in the removal of surplusage, from the last finish of the gem-engraver blowing away the last particle of invisible dust, back to the earliest divination of the finished work to be, lying somewhere, according to Michel- angelo's fancy, in the rough-hewn block of stone." That the literary artist tests his skill by a masterly omission of all that is better left unsaid is a truth widely admitted and scantily utilized. Authors who have not taken the trouble *de faire leur toilette* admit

us with painful frankness into their dressing-
rooms, and suffer us to gaze more intimately
than is agreeable to us upon the dubious
mysteries of their deshabille.   Authors who
have the gift of continuity disregard with
insistent generosity the limits of time and
patience.   What a noble poem was lost to
myriads of readers when "The Ring and the
Book" reached its twenty thousandth line!
How inexorable is the tyranny of a great and
powerful poet who will spare his readers nothing!   Authors who are indifferent to the
beauties of reserve charge down upon us with
a dreadful impetuosity from which there is no
escape.   The strength that lies in delicacy,
the chasteness of style which does not abandon itself to every impulse, are qualities ill-
understood by men who subordinate taste to
fervor, and whose words, coarse, rank, or unc-
tuous, betray the undisciplined intellect that
mistakes passion for power.   "The language
of poets," says Shelley, "has always effected a
certain uniform and harmonious recurrence of
sound, without which it were not poetry;" and
it is the sustained effort to secure this balanced harmony, this magnificent work within

limits, which constitutes the achievement of the poet, and gives beauty and dignity to his art. " Where is the man who can flatter himself that he knows the language of prose, if he has not assiduously practiced the language of poetry? " asks M. Francisque Sarcey, whose requirements are needlessly exacting, but whose views would have been cordially indorsed by at least one great master of English. Dryden always maintained that the admirable quality of his prose was due to his long training in a somewhat mechanical verse. A more modern and diverting approximation of M. Sarcey's views may be found in the robust statement of Benjamin Franklin : " I approved, for my part, the amusing one's self now and then with poetry, so far as to improve one's language, but no farther." It is a pity that people cannot always be born in the right generation ! What a delicious picture is presented to our fancy of a nineteenth-century Franklin amusing himself and improving his language by an occasional study of " Sordello " !

The absolute mastery of words, which is the prerogative of genius, can never be acquired

by painstaking, or revealed to criticism.   Mr.
Lowell, pondering deeply on the subject, has
devoted whole pages to a scholarly analysis of
the causes which assisted Shakespeare to his
unapproached and unapproachable vocabulary.
The English language was then, Mr. Lowell
reminds us, a living thing, " hot from the
hearts and brains of a people ; not hardened
yet, but moltenly ductile to new shapes of
sharp and clear relief in the moulds of new
thought.   Shakespeare found words ready to
his use, original and untarnished, types of
thought whose edges were unworn by repeated
impressions. . . . No arbitrary line had been
drawn between high words and low ; vulgar
then meant simply what was common ; poetry
had not been aliened from the people by the
establishment of an Upper House of vocables.
The conception of the poet had no time to cool
while he was debating the comparative respec-
tability of this phrase or that ; but he snatched
what word his instinct prompted, and saw no
indiscretion in making a king speak as his
country nurse might have taught him."

It is a curious thing, however, that the more
we try to account for the miracles of genius,

the more miraculous they grow. We can never hope to understand the secret of Homer's style. It is best to agree simply with Mr. Pater : "Homer was always saying things in this manner." We can never know how Keats came to write,

"With beaded bubbles winking at the brim,"

or those other lines, perhaps the most beautiful in our language,

"Magic casements, opening on the foam
Of perilous seas, in faery lands forlorn."

It is all a mystery, hidden from the uninspired, and Mr. Lowell's clean-built scaffolding, while it helps us to a comprehensive enjoyment of Shakespeare, leaves us dumb and amazed as ever before the concentrated splendor of a single line, —

"In cradle of the rude, imperious surge."

There is only one way to fathom its conception. The great waves reared their foamy heads, and whispered him the words.

The richness of Elizabethan English, the freedom and delight with which men sounded and explored the charming intricacies of a tongue that was expanding daily into fresh

majesty and beauty, must have given to literature some of the allurements of navigation.
Mariners sailed away upon stormy seas, on
strange, half-hinted errands; haunted by the
shadow of glory, dazzled by the lustre of
wealth. Scholars ventured far upon the unknown ocean of letters; haunted by the seduc-
tions of prose, dazzled by the fairness of
verse. They brought back curious spoils,
gaudy, subtle, sumptuous, according to the
taste or potency of the discoverer. Their
words have often a mingled weight and sweetness, whether conveying briefly a single
thought, like Burton's "touched with the
loadstone of love," or adding strength and
lustre to the ample delineations of Ben Jon-
son. "Give me that wit whom praise excites, glory puts on, or disgrace grieves; he
is to be nourished with ambition, pricked forward with honors, checked with reprehension,
and never to be suspected of sloth." Bacon's
admirable conciseness, in which nothing is
disregarded, but where every word carries its
proper value and expresses its exact significance, is equaled only by Cardinal Newman.
"Reading maketh a full man, conference a

ready man, and study an exact man," says
Bacon ; and this simple accuracy of definition
reminds us inevitably of the lucid terseness
with which every sentence of the " Apologia "
reveals the thought it holds. " The truest
expedience is to answer right out when you
are asked ; the wisest economy is to have no
management; the best prudence is not to be a
coward." As for the *naïveté* and the picturesqueness which lend such inexpressible charm
to the earlier writers and atone for so many of
their misdeeds, what can be more agreeable
than to hear Sir Walter Raleigh remark with
cheerful ingenuousness, " Some of our cap-
taines garoused of wine till they were reasonable pleasant " ! — a most engaging way of
narrating a not altogether uncommon occur-
rence. And what can be more winning to the
ear than the simple grace with which Roger
Ascham writes of familiar things : " In the
whole year, Springtime, Summer, Fall of the
Leaf, and Winter; and in one day, Morning,
Noontime, Afternoon, and Eventide, altereth
the course of the weather, the pith of the bow,
the strength of the man " ! It seems an easy
thing to say " fall of the leaf " for fall, and

" eventide " for evening, but in such easy
things lies the subtle beauty of language ; in
the rejection of such nice distinctions lies the
barrenness of common speech. We can hardly
spare the time, in these hurried days, to
speak of the fall of the leaf, to use four words
where one would suffice, merely because the
four words have a graceful significance, and
the one word has none; and so, even in composition, this finely colored phrase, with its
hint of russet, wind-swept woods, is lost to us
forever. Yet compare with it the line which
Lord Tennyson, that great master of beautiful words, puts into Marian's song: —

> " ' Have you still any honey, my dear ? '
> She said, ' It 's the fall of the year ;
> But come, come ! ' "

How tame and gray is the idiom which conveys a fact, which defines a season, but suggests nothing to our imaginations, by the side
of the idiom which brings swiftly before our
eyes the brilliant desolation of autumn !

The narrow vocabulary, which is the conver-
sational freehold of people whose education
should have provided them a broader field,
admits of little that is picturesque or forcible,

and of less that is finely graded or delicately conceived. Ordinary conversation appears to consist mainly of " ands," " buts," and " thes," with an occasional " well " to give a flavor of nationality, a " yes " or " no " to stand for individual sentiment, and a few widely exaggerated terms to destroy value and perspective.

Is this, one wonders, the " treasure of dexterous felicities " which Mr. Bagehot contemplated with such delight, and which a critical society is destined to preserve flawless and uncontaminated? Is this the " heroic utterance," the great " mother tongue," possessing which we all become — or so Mr. Sydney Dobell assures us —

" Lords of an empire wide as Shakespeare's soul,
　Sublime as Milton's immemorial theme,
　And rich as Chaucer's speech and fair as Spenser's dream " ?

Is this the element whose beauty excites Mr. Oscar Wilde to such rapturous and finely worded praise, — praise which awakens in us a noble emulation to prove what we can accomplish with a medium at once so sumptuous and so flexible ? " For the material that painter or sculptor uses is meagre in comparison with language," says Mr. Wilde. " Words have not merely music as sweet as that of viol and lute, color as rich and vivid as any that makes lovely for us the canvas of the Venetian or the Spaniard, and plastic form no less sure and certain than that which reveals itself in marble or in bronze; but thought and passion and spirituality are theirs also, are theirs indeed alone. If the Greeks had criticised nothing but language, they would still have been the great art critics of the world. To know the principles of the highest art is to know the principles of all the arts."

This is not claiming too much, for in truth Mr. Wilde is sufficiently well equipped to illustrate his claim. If his sentences are sometimes overloaded with ornament, the decorations are gold, not tinsel; if his vocabulary is gorgeous, it is never glaring; if his allusions are fanciful, they are controlled and subdued into moderation. Even the inevitable and swiftly uttered reproach of " fine writing " cannot altogether blind us to the fact that his are beautiful words, — pearls and amethysts M. Gautier would call them, — aptly chosen, and fitted into place with the careful skill of a goldsmith. They are

free, moreover, from that vice of unexpected-
ness which is part of fine writing, and which
Mr. Saintsbury finds so prevalent among the
literary workers of to-day ; the desire to surprise us by some new and profoundly ir-
relevant application of a familiar word. The
" veracity " of a bar of music, the finely exe-
cuted " passage " of a marble chimney-piece,
the " andante " of a sonnet, and the curious
statement, commonly applied to Mr. Glad-
stone, that he is " part of the conscience of
a nation," — these are the vagaries which to
Mr. Saintsbury, and to every other student
of words, appear so manifestly discouraging.
Mr. James Payn tells a pleasant story of an
æsthetic sideboard which was described to
him as having a Chippendale feeling about
it, before which touching conceit the ever
famous " fringes of the north star " pale into
insignificance. A recent editor of Shelley's
letters and essays says with seeming seriousness in his preface that the " Witch of Atlas "
is a " characteristic outcome," an " exquisite
mouse of fancy brought forth by what mountain of Shelleyan imagination." Now, when
a careful student and an appreciative reader

can bring himself to speak of a poem as a "mouse of fancy," merely for the sake of forcing a conceit, and confronting us with the perils of the unexpected, it is time we turned soberly back to first principles and to our dictionaries; it is time we listened anew to M. Gautier's advice, and studied the value of words.

ENNUI.

"Tous les genres sont permis, hors le genre ennuyeux."

"WANT and ennui," says Schopenhauer,
" are the two poles of human life." The further we escape from one evil, the nearer we
inevitably draw to the other. As soon as the
first rude pressure of necessity is relieved, and
man has leisure to think of something beyond
his unsatisfied craving for food and shelter,
then ennui steps in and claims him for her
own. It is the price he pays, not merely for
luxury, but for comfort. Time, the inexorable
taskmaster of poor humanity, drives us hard
with whip and spur when we are struggling
under the heavy burden of work ; but stays his
hand, and prolongs the creeping hours, when
we are delivered over to that weariness of
spirit which weights each moment with lead.
Time is, in fact, either our open oppressor or
our false friend. He is that agent by which,
at every instant, " all things in our hands

become as nothing, and lose any real value
they possess."

Here is a doctrine distinctly discouraging,
and stated with that relentless candor which
compels our reluctant consideration. There
can be no doubt that to Schopenhauer's mind
ennui was an evil every whit as palpable as
want. He hated and feared them both with
the painful susceptibility of a self-centred
man ; and he strove resolutely from his youth
to protect himself against these twin disasters
of life. The determined fashion in which he
guarded his patrimony from loss resembled the
determined fashion in which he strove — with
less success — to guard himself from boredom.
The vapid talk, the little wearisome iterations,
which most of us bear resignedly enough because custom has taught us patience, were to
him intolerable afflictions. He retaliated by
an ungracious dismissal of society as something pitiably and uniformly contemptible.
His advice has not the grave and simple wisdom of Sir Thomas Browne, " Be able to be
alone," but is founded rather on Voltaire's dis-
dainful maxim, " The world is full of people
who are not worth speaking to," and implies

an almost savage rejection of one's fellow-beings. "Every fool is pathetically social," says
Schopenhauer, and the advantage of solitude
consists less in the possession of ourselves than
in the escape from others. With whimsical
eagerness he built barrier after barrier between himself and the dreaded enemy, ennui,
only to see his citadel repeatedly stormed, and
to find himself at the mercy of his foe. There
is but one method, after all, by which the in-
vader can be even partially disarmed, and this
method was foreign to Schopenhauer's nature.
It was practiced habitually by Sir Walter
Scott, who, in addition to his sustained and
splendid work, threw himself with such unself-
ish, unswerving ardor into the interests of
his brother men that he never gave them a
thorough chance to bore him. They did their
part stoutly enough, and were doubtless as
tiresome as they knew how to be; but his invincible sweet temper triumphed over their
malignity, and enabled him to say, in the evening of his life, that he had suffered little at
their hands, and had seldom found any one
from whom he could not extract either amusement or edification.

Perhaps his journal tells a different tale, a tale of heavy moments stretching into hours, and borne with cheerful patience out of simple consideration for others. Men and women, friends and strangers, took forcible possession of his golden leisure, and he yielded it to them without a murmur. That which was well-nigh maddening to Carlyle's irritable nerves and selfish petulance, and which strained even Charles Lamb's forbearance to the snapping-point, Sir Walter endured smilingly, as if it were the most reasonable thing in the world. Mr. Lang is right when he says Scott did not preach socialism, he practiced it; that is, he never permitted himself to assign to his own comfort or convenience a very important place in existence; he never supposed his own satisfaction to be the predestined purpose of the universe. But his love for genial life, his keen enjoyment of social pleasures, made him singularly sensitive to ennui. He was able, indeed, like Sir Thomas Browne, to be alone, — when the charity of his fellow-creatures suffered it, — and he delighted in diverting companionship, whether of peers or hinds; but the weariness of daily intercourse with stupid people told as heavily upon him as upon less patient victims. Little notes scattered throughout his journal reveal his misery, and awaken sympathetic echoes in every long-tried soul. "Of all bores," he writes, "the greatest is to hear a dull and bashful man sing a facetious song." And again, with humorous intensity: "Miss Ayton's father is a bore, after the fashion of all fathers, mothers, aunts, and other chaperons of pretty actresses." And again, this time in a hasty scrawl to Ballantyne: —

"Oh, James! oh, James! two Irish dames
    Oppress me very sore :
I groaning send one sheet I 've penned,
    For, hang them! there 's no more."

That Sir Walter forgot his sufferings as soon as they were over is proof, not of callousness, but of magnanimity. He forgave his tormentors the instant they ceased to torment him, and then found time to deplore his previous irritation. "I might at least have asked him to dinner," he was heard murmuring self-reproachfully, when an unscrupulous intruder had at last departed from Abbotsford; and on another occasion, when some impatient lads refused to emulate his forbearance, he recalled them with prompt insistence to their forgotten sense of propriety. " Come, come, young gentlemen," he expostulated. " It requires no small ability, I assure you, to be a decided bore. You must endeavor to show a little more respect."

The self-inflicted pangs of ennui are less salutary and infinitely more onerous than those we suffer at the hands of others. It is natural that our just resentment when people weary us should result in a temporary taste for solitude, a temporary exaltation of our own society. Like most sentiments erected on an airy trestle-work of vanity, this is an agreeable delusion while it lasts ; but it seldom does last after we are bold enough to put it to the test. The inevitable and rational discontent which lies at the bottom of our hearts is not a thing to be banished by noise, or lulled to sleep by silence. We are not sufficient for ourselves, and companionship is not sufficient for us. " Venez, monsieur," said Louis XIII. to a listless courtier ; " allons nous ennuyer ensemble." We fancy it is the detail of life, its small grievances, its apparent monotony, its fretful cares, its hours alternately lagging and feverish, that wear out the joy of existence. This is not so. Were each day differently filled, the result would be much the same. Young Maurice de Guérin, struggling with a depression he too clearly understands, strikes at the very root of the matter in one dejected sentence : " Mon Dieu, que je souffre de la vie ! Non dans ses accidents, un peu de philosophie y suffit ; mais dans elle-même, dans sa substance, à part tout phénomène." To which the steadfast optimist opposes an admirable retort : " It is a pity that M. de Guérin should have permitted himself this relentless analysis of a misery which is never bettered by contemplation." Happiness may not be, as we are sometimes told, the legacy of the barbarian, but neither is it a final outcome of civilization. Men can weary, and do weary, of every stage that represents a step in the world's progress, and the ennui of mental starvation is equaled only by the ennui of mental satiety.

It is curious how much of this temper is reflected in the somewhat dispiriting literature which attains popularity to-day. Mr. Hamlin Garland, whose leaden-hued sketches called — I think unfairly — " Main-Travelled Roads " have deprived most of us of some cheerful hours, paints with an unfaltering hand a life in which ennui sits enthroned. It is not the poverty of his Western farmers that oppresses us. Real biting poverty, which withers lesser evils with its deadly breath, is not known to these people at all. They have roofs, fire, food, and clothing. It is not the ceaseless labor, the rough fare, the gray skies, the muddy barnyards, which stand for the trouble in their lives. It is the dreadful weariness of living. It is the burden of a dull existence, clogged at every pore, and the hopeless melancholy of which they have sufficient intelligence to understand. Theirs is the ennui of emptiness, and the implied reproach on every page is that a portion, and only a portion, of mankind is doomed to walk along these shaded paths; while happier mortals who abide in New York, or perhaps in Paris, spend their days in a pleasant tumult of intellectual and artistic excitation. The clearest denial of this fallacy may be found in that matchless and desolate sketch of Mr. Pater's called "Sebastian van Storck," where we have painted for us with penetrating distinctness man's deliberate rejection of those crowded accessories which, to the empty-handed, represent the joys of life. Never has the undying essence of ennui been revealed to our unwilling gaze as in this merciless picture. Never has it been so portrayed in its awful nakedness, amid a plenty which it cannot be persuaded to share. We see the rich, warm, highly colored surroundings, the vehement intensity of work and pastime, the artistic completeness of every detail, the solicitations of love, the delicate and alluring touches which give to every day its separate delight, its individual value; and, amid all these things, the impatient soul striving vainly to adjust itself to a life which seems so worth the living. Here, indeed, is one of " Fortune's favorites," whom she decks with garlands like a sacrificial heifer, and at whom, unseen, she points her mocking finger. Encompassed from childhood by the " thriving genius " of the Dutch, by the restless activity which made dry land and populous towns where nature had willed the sea, and by the admirable art which added each year to the heaped-up treasures of Holland, Sebastian van Storck has but one vital impulse which shapes itself to an end, — escape ; escape from an existence made unendurable by its stifling fullness, its vivid and marvelous accomplishment.

It is an interesting question to determine, or to endeavor to determine, how far animals share man's melancholy capacity for ennui. Schopenhauer, who, like Hartmann and all other professional pessimists, steadfastly maintains that beasts are happier than men, is disposed to believe that in their natural state they never suffer from this malady, and that, even when domesticated, only the most intelligent give any indication of its presence. But how does Schopenhauer know that which he so confidently affirms? The bird, impelled by an instinct she is powerless to resist, sits patiently on her eggs until they are hatched; but who can say she is not weary of the pastime ? What loneliness and discontent may find expression in the lion's dreadful roar, which is said to be as mournful as it is terrible ! We are naturally tempted, in moments of fretfulness and dejection, to seek relief — not unmixed with envy — in contemplating with Sir Thomas Browne " the happiness of inferior creatures

who in tranquillity possess their constitutions."
But freedom from care, and from the apprehension that is worse than care, does not necessarily imply freedom from all disagreeable
sensations ; and the surest claim of the brute
to satisfaction, its absolute adequacy to the
place it is designed to fill, is destroyed by our
interference in its behalf. As a result, domestic pets reveal plainly to every close observer
how frequently they suffer from ennui. They
pay, in smaller coin, the same price that man
pays for comfortable living. Mr. Ruskin has
written with ready sympathy of the house dog,
who bears resignedly long hours of dull inaction, and only shows by his frantic delight
what a relief it is to be taken out for the mild
dissipation of a stroll. I have myself watched
and pitied the too evident ennui of my cat,
poor little beast of prey, deprived in a mouse-
less home of the supreme pleasures of the
hunt ; fed until dinner ceases to be a coveted
enjoyment ; housed, cushioned, combed, ca-
ressed, and forced to bear upon her pretty
shoulders the burden of a wearisome opulence,
— or what represents opulence to a pussy. I
have seen Agrippina listlessly moving from

chair to chair, and from sofa to sofa, in a vain
attempt to nap; looking for a few languid
minutes out of the window with the air of a
great lady sadly bored at the play; and then
turning dejectedly back into the room whose
attractions she had long since exhausted. Her
expressive eyes lifted to mine betrayed her discontent; the lassitude of an irksome luxury
unnerved her graceful limbs; if she could have
spoken, it would have been to complain with
Charles Lamb of that " dumb, soporifical good-
for-nothingness " which clogs the wheels of
life.

It is a pleasant fancy, baseless and proof-
less, which makes us imagine the existence of
fishes to be peculiarly tranquil and unmolested.
The element in which they live appears to
shelter them from so many evils; noises especially, and the sharpness of sudden change,
scorching heats, and the inclement skies of
winter. A delightful mystery wraps them
round, and the smooth apathy with which they
glide through the water suggests content ap-
proaching to complacency. That old-fashioned
poem beginning

" Deep in the wave is a coral grove,
Where the purple mullet and goldfish rove,"

filled my childish heart with a profound envy
of these happy creatures, which was greatly
increased by reading a curious story of Father
Faber's, called "The Melancholy Heart." In
this tale, a little shipwrecked girl is carried to
the depths of the ocean, and sees the green sea
swinging to and fro because it is so full of joy,
and the fishes waving their glistening fins in
silent satisfaction, and the oysters opening and
shutting their shells in lazy raptures of delight.
Afterwards she visits the birds and beasts and
insects, and finds amongst them intelligence,
industry, patience, ingenuity, — a whole host
of admirable qualities, — but nowhere else the
sweet contentment of that dumb watery life.
So universal is this fallible sentiment that
even Leopardi, while assigning to all created
things their full share of pain, reluctantly admits that the passive serenity of the less viva-
cious creatures of the sea — starfish and their
numerous brothers and sisters — is the nearest
possible approach to an utterly impossible
happiness. And indeed it is difficult to look
at a sea-urchin slowly moving its countless
spines in the clear shallow water without
thinking that here, at least, is an existence

equally free from excitability and from ennui; here is a state of being sufficient for itself, and embracing all the enjoyment it can hold. The other side of the story is presented when we discover the little prickly cup lying empty and dry on the peak of a neighboring rock, and know that a crow's sharp beak has relentlessly dug the poor urchin from its comfortable cradle, and ended its slumbrous felicity. Yet the sudden cessation of life has nothing whatever to do with its reasonable contentment. The question is, not how soon is it over, or how does it come to an end, but is it worth living while it lasts? Moreover, the chances of death make the sweetness of self-preservation; and this is precisely the sentiment which Leigh Hunt has so admirably embodied in those lines — the finest, I think, he ever wrote — where the fish pleads for its own pleasant and satisfactory existence : —

> " A cold, sweet, silver life, wrapped in round waves,
> Quickened with touches of transporting fear."

Here, as elsewhere, fear is the best antidote for ennui. The early settlers of America, surrounded by hostile Indians, and doubtful each morning whether the coming nightfall would

not see their rude homes given to the flames,
probably suffered but little from the dullness
which seems so oppressive to the peaceful agri-
culturist of to-day. The mediæval women, who
were content to pass their time in weaving
endless tapestries, had less chance to complain
of the monotony of life than their artistic,
scientific, literary, and philanthropic sisters of
our age; for at any hour, breaking in upon
their tranquil labors, might be heard the
trumpet's blast; at any hour might come the
tidings, good or bad, which meant a few more
years of security, or the horrors of siege and
pillage.

It is pleasant to turn our consideration from
the ennui which is inevitable, and consequently
tragic, to the ennui which is accidental, and
consequently diverting. The first is part of
ourselves, from which there is no escape; the
second is, as a rule, the contribution of our
neighbors, and may be eluded if fortune and
our own wits favor us. Lord Byron, for example, finding himself hard beset by Madame
de Staël, whom he abhorred, had the dexterity
to entrap poor little " Monk " Lewis into the
conversation, and then slipped away from both,

leaving them the dismally congenial task of wearying each other without mercy. "A bore," says Bishop Selwyn, "is a man who will persist in talking about himself when you want to talk about yourself;" and this simple explanation offers a satisfactory solution of much of the ennui suffered in society. People with theories of life are, perhaps, the most relentless of their kind, for no time or place is sacred from their devastating elucidations. A theoretic socialist — not the practical working kind, like Sir Walter — is adamant to the fatigue of his listeners. "Eloquence," says Mr. Lowell feelingly, "has no bowels for its victims;" and one of the most pathetic figures in the history of literature is poor Heine, awakened from his sweet morning nap by Ludwig Börne, who sat relentlessly on the edge of the bed and talked patriotism. I hardly think that even this wanton injury justified Heine in his cruel attack upon Börne, when the latter was dead and could offer no defense; yet who knows how many drops of concentrated bitterness were stored up in those dreary moments of boredom! The only other instance of ennui which seems as grievous and as cruel is the picture of the Baron Fouqué's brilliant wife condemned to play loto every evening with the officers of the victorious French army; an illustration equally novel and malign of the devastating inhumanity of war.

In fact, amusements which do not amuse are among the most depressing of earthly evils. When Sir George Cornwall Lewis candidly confessed that life would be tolerable were it not for its pleasures, he had little notion that he was uttering a witticism fated to enjoy a melancholy immortality. His protest was purely personal, and society, prompt to recognize a grievance when it is presented, has gone on ever since peevishly and monotonously echoing his lament. We crave diversion so eagerly, we need it so sorely, that our disappointment in its elusiveness is fed by the flickerings of perpetual hope. Ennui has been defined as a desire for activity without the capacity for action, as a state of inertia quickened by discontent. But it is rather a desire for amusement than for activity; it is a rational instinct warped by the irony of circumstances, and by our own selfish limitations. It was not activity that Schopenhauer lacked. He worked

hard all his life, and with the concentrated
industry of a man who knew exactly what
he wanted to do. It was the common need of
enjoyment, which he shared with the rest of
mankind, and his own singular incapacity for
enjoying himself, which chafed him into bitterness, and made him so unreasonably angry with
the world. " In human existence," says Leopardi, " the intervals between pleasure and
pain are occupied by ennui. And since all
pleasures are like cobwebs, exceedingly fragile,
thin, and transparent, ennui penetrates their
tissue and saturates them, just as air penetrates the webs. It is, indeed, nothing but a
yearning for happiness, without the illusion of
pleasure or the reality of pain. This yearning
is never satisfied, since true happiness does not
exist. So that life is interwoven with weariness
and suffering, and one of these evils disap-
pears only to give place to the other. Such is
the destiny of man."

Now, to endure pain resolutely, courage is
required ; to endure ennui, one must be bred
to the task. The restraints of a purely artificial society are sufferable to those only whom
custom has rendered docile, and who have been

trained to subordinate their own impulses and
desires. The more elaborate the social conditions, the more relentless this need of adjustment, which makes a harmonious whole at
the cost of individual development. We all
know how, when poor Frances Burney was
lifted suddenly from the cheerful freedom of
middle-class life to the wearisome etiquette of
a court, she drooped and fretted under the burden of an honor which brought her nothing
but vexation. Macaulay, who champions her
cause with burning zeal, is pleased to represent the monotony of court as simple slavery
with no extenuating circumstances. He likens
Dr. Burney conducting his daughter to the
palace to a Circassian father selling his own
child into bondage. The sight of the authoress
of "Evelina" assisting at the queen's toilet, or
chatting sleepily with the ladies in waiting,
thrills him with indignation; the thought of
her playing cards night after night with
Madame Schwellenberg reduces him to despair. And indeed, card-playing, if you have
not the grace to like it, is the most unprofitable form of social martyrdom; you suffer
horribly yourself, and you add very little to

the pleasure of your neighbor. The Baroness Fouqué may have conquered the infantine imbecilities of loto with no great mental exhaustion. If she were painfully bored, her patience alone was taxed. The Frenchmen probably thought her a pleased and animated companion. But Miss Burney, delicate, sleepy, fatigued, loathing cards, and inwardly rebellious at her fate, must have made the game drag sadly before bedtime. It was a dreary waste of moments for her; but a less intolerant partisan than Macaulay would have some sympathy to spare for poor Madame Schwellenberg, who, like most women of rank, adored the popular pastime, and who doubtless found the distinguished young novelist a very unsatisfactory associate.

It is salutary to turn from Miss Burney and her wrathful historian to the letters of Charlotte Elizabeth, mother of the Regent d'Orléans, and see how the oppressive monotony of the French court was cheerfully endured for fifty years by a woman exiled from home and kindred, whose pleasures were few, whose annoyances were manifold. Madame would have enjoyed nothing better than a bowl of beer,

soup, or a dish of sausages eaten in congenial
company. She lunched daily alone, on hated
French messes, stared at by twenty footmen,
from whose supercilious eyes she was glad to
escape with hunger still unsatisfied. Madame
detested sermons. She listened to them end-
lessly without complaint, and was grateful for
the occasional privilege of a nap. Madame
liked cards. She was not permitted to play,
nor even to show herself at the lansquenet
table. She never gambled, — in fact, she had
no money, — and it was a fancy of her husband's that she brought him ill luck by hover-
ing near. Neither was she allowed to retire.
" All the old women who do not play have to
be entertained by me," she writes with sur-
passing good humor. " This goes on from
seven to ten, and makes me yawn frightfully."
Supper was eaten at the royal table, where the
guests often waited three quarters of an hour
for the king to appear, and where nobody
spoke a word during the meal. " I live as
though I were quite alone in the world," confesses this friendless exile to her favorite
correspondent, the Raugravine Louise. " But
I am resigned to such a state of things, and

I meddle in nothing." Here was a woman
trained to the endurance of ennui. The theatre
and the chase were her sole amusements; letter-writing was her only occupation. Her
healthy German nature had in it no trace of
languor, no bitterness born of useless rebellion
against fate. She knew how to accept the inevitable, and how to enjoy the accidental; and
this double philosophy afforded her something
closely resembling content. Napoleon, it is
said, once desired some comedians to play
at court, and M. de Talleyrand gravely an-
nounced to the audience waiting to hear them,
"Gentlemen, the emperor earnestly requests
you to be amused." Had Charlotte Elizabeth
—long before laid to sleep in St. Denis—
been one of that patient group, she would have
literally obeyed the royal commands. She
would have responded with prompt docility to
any offered entertainment. This is not an easy
task. "Amuse me, if you can find out how to
do it," was the melancholy direction of Riche-
lieu to Boisrobert, when the pains of ennui
grew unbearable, and even kittens ceased to
be diverting. Amuse! amuse! amuse! is the
plea of a weariness as wide as the world, and

as old as humanity. Amuse me for a little while, that I may think I have escaped from myself.

It is curious that England should have to borrow from France the word " ennui," while the French are unanimous in their opinion that the thing itself is emphatically of English growth. The old rhyme,

" Jean Rosbif écuyer,
Qui pendit soi-même pour se désennuyer,"

has never lost its application, though the present generation of English-speaking men are able to digest a great deal of dullness without seeking such violent forms of relief. In fact, Mr. Oscar Wilde, prompt to offer an unwelcome criticism, explains the amazing popularity of the psychological and religiously irreligious novel on the ground that the *genre ennuyeux*, which no Frenchman can bring himself to pardon, is the one form of literature which his countrymen thoroughly enjoy. They have a kindly tolerance for stupid people as well, and the ill-natured term " bore " has only forced itself of late years upon an urbane and long-suffering public. Johnson's dictionary is innocent of the word, though Johnson himself was well acquainted with the article. As late as 1822, a reviewer in "Colburn's Magazine" entreats his readers to use the word " bore ; " to write it, if they please ; to print it, even, if necessary. Why shrink from the expression, when the creature itself is so common, and "daily gaining ground in the country " ?

Before this date, however, one English writer had given to literature some priceless illustrations of the species. "Could we but study our bores as Miss Austen must have studied hers in her country village," says Mrs. Ritchie, "what a delightful world this might be!" But I seriously doubt whether any real enjoyment could be extracted from Miss Bates, or Mr. Rushworth, or Sir William Lucas, in the flesh. If we knew them, we should probably feel precisely as did Emma Woodhouse, and Maria Bertram, and Elizabeth Bennet, — vastly weary of their company. In fact, only their brief appearances make the two gentlemen bores so diverting, even in fiction ; and Miss Bates, I must confess, taxes my patience sorely. She is so tiresome that she tires, and I am invariably tempted to do

what her less fortunate townspeople would have
gladly done, — run away from her to more
congenial society. Surely comedy ceases, and
tragedy begins, when poor Jane Fairfax es-
capes from the strawberry party at Donwell,
and seeks, under the burning noonday sun,
the blessed relief of solitude. "We all know
at times what it is to be wearied in spirits.
Mine, I admit, are exhausted," is the confession wrung from the silent lips of a girl who
has borne all that human nature can bear
from Miss Bates's affectionate solicitude. Perhaps the best word ever spoken upon the creation of such characters in novels comes from
Cardinal Newman. "It is very difficult," he
says, "to delineate a bore in a narrative, for
the simple reason that he is a bore. A tale
must aim at condensation, but a bore acts in
solution. It is only in the long run that he
is ascertained." And when he *is* ascertained,
and his identity established beyond reach of
doubt, what profit have we in his desolating
perfections? Miss Austen was far from enjoying the dull people whom she knew in life.
We have the testimony of her letters to this
effect. Has not Mrs. Stent, otherwise lost to

fame, been crowned with direful immortality as the woman who bored Jane Austen? "We may come to be Mrs. Stents ourselves," she writes, with facile self-reproach at her impatience, "unequal to anything, and unwelcome to anybody;" an apprehension manifestly manufactured out of nothingness to strengthen some wavering purpose of amendment. Stupidity is acknowledged to be the one natural gift which cannot be cultivated, and Miss Austen well knew it lay beyond her grasp. With as much sincerity could Emma Woodhouse have said, "I may come in time to be a second Miss Bates."

There is a small, compact, and enviable minority among us, who, through no merit of their own, are incapable of being bored, and consequently escape the endless pangs of ennui. They are so clearly recognized as a body that a great deal of the world's work is prepared especially for their entertainment and instruction. Books are written for them, sermons are preached to them, lectures are given to them, papers are read to them, societies and clubs are organized for them, discussions after the order of Melchizedek are carried on

monotonously in their behalf. A brand new
school of fiction has been invented for their
exclusive diversion; and several complicated
systems of religion have been put together for
their recent edification. It is hardly a matter
of surprise that, fed on such meats, they
should wax scornful, and deride their hungry
fellow-creatures. It is even less amazing that
these fellow-creatures should weary from time
to time of the crumbs that fall from their
table. It is told of Pliny the younger that,
being invited to a dinner, he consented to come
on the express condition that the conversation
should abound in Socratic discourses. Here
was a man equally insensible to ennui and to
the sufferings of others. The guests at that
ill-starred banquet appear to have been sacrificed as ruthlessly as the fish and game they
ate. They had not even the loophole of escape
which Mr. Bagehot contemplates so admir-
ingly in Paradise Lost. Whenever Adam's
remarks expand too obviously into a sermon,
Eve, in the most discreet and wife-like manner,
steps softly away, and refreshes herself with
slumber. Indeed, when we come to think of
it, conversation between these two must have

been difficult at times, because they had nobody to talk about. If we exiled our neighbors permanently from our discussions, we
should soon be reduced to silence ; and if we
confined ourselves even to laudatory remarks,
we should probably say but little. Miss Frances Power Cobbe, who is uncompromisingly
hostile to the feeble vices of society, insists
that it is the duty of every woman to look
bored when she hears a piece of scandal ; but
this mandate is hardly in accord with Miss
Cobbe's other requisite for true womanhood,
absolute and undeviating sincerity. How can
she look bored when she does not feel bored,
unless she plays the hypocrite? And while
many women are shocked and repelled by
scandal, few, alas! are wont to find it tiresome. I have not even observed any exceeding weariness in men when subjected to a
similar ordeal. In that pitiless dialogue of
Landor's between Catherine of Russia and
Princess Dashkov, we find some opinions on
this subject stated with appalling candor.
"Believe me," says the empress, "there is
nothing so delightful in life as to find a liar in
a person of repute. Have you never heard

good folks rejoicing at it? Or rather, can you
mention to me any one who has not been in
raptures when he could communicate such
glad tidings? The goutiest man would go on
foot to tell his friend of it at midnight; and
would cross the Neva for the purpose, when
he doubted whether the ice would bear him."
Here, indeed, is the very soul and essence of
ennui; not the virtuous sentiment which re-
volts at the disclosure of another's faults, but
that deep and deadly ennui of life which wel-
comes evil as a distraction. The same selfish
lassitude which made the gladiatorial combats
a pleasant sight for the jaded eyes which witnessed them finds relief for its tediousness to-
day in the swift destruction of confidence and
reputation.

There is a curious and melancholy fable of
Leopardi's in which he seeks to explain what
always puzzled him sorely, the continued endurance of life. In the beginning, he says,
the gods gave to men an existence without
care, and an earth without evil. The world
was small, and easily traversed. No seas divided it, no mountains rose frowning from its
bosom, no extremes of heat or cold afflicted

its inhabitants. Their wants were supplied, their pleasures provided; their happiness, Jove thought, assured. For a time all things went well; but as the human race outgrew its infancy, it tired of this smooth perfection, and little by little there dawned upon men the inherent worthlessness of life. Every day they sounded its depths more clearly, and every day they wearied afresh of all they knew and were. Illusions vanished, and the insupportable pains of ennui forced them to cast aside a gift in which they found no value. They desired death, and sought it at their own hands.

Then Jove, half in wrath and half in pity, devised a means by which his rebellious creatures might be preserved. He enlarged the earth, moulded the mountains, and poured into mighty hollows the restless and pitiless seas. Burning heat and icy cold he sent, diseases and dangers of every kind, craving desires that could never be satisfied, vain ambitions, a babble of many tongues, and the deep-rooted animosities of nations. Gone was the old tranquillity, vanished the old ennui. A new race, struggling amid terrible hardships, fought bravely and bitterly for the preservation of an existence they had formerly despised. Man found his life filled with toil, sweetened by peril, checked by manifold disasters, and was deluded into cherishing at any cost that which was so painful to sustain. The greater the difficulties and dangers, the more he opposed to them his own indomitable purpose, the more determined he was to live. The zest of perpetual effort, the keenness of contention, the brief, sweet triumph over adversity, — these left him neither the time nor the disposition to question the value of all that he wrung from fate.

It is a cheerless philosophy, but not without value to the sanguine socialist of to-day, who dreams of preparing for all of us a lifetime of unbroken ennui.

It is dubious wisdom to walk in the footprints of a giant, and to stumble with little steps along the road where his great strides were taken. Yet many years have passed since Hazlitt trod this way; fresh flowers have grown by the route, and fresh weeds have fought with them for mastery. The face of the country has changed for better or for worse, and a brief survey reveals much that never met his eyes. The journey, too, was safer in his day than in ours; and while he gathers and analyzes every species of wit and humor, it plainly does not occur to him for a moment that either calls for any protection at his hands. Hazlitt is so sure that laughter is our inalienable right, that he takes no pains to soften its cadences or to justify its mirth. "We laugh at that in others which is a serious matter to ourselves," he says, and sees no reason why this should not be. " Some one is

generally sure to be the sufferer by a joke;"
and, fortified with this assurance, he confesses
to a frank delight in the comic parts of the
Arabian Nights, although recognizing keenly
the spirit of cruelty that underlies them, and
aware that they "carry the principle of callous
indifference in a jest as far as it can go."
Don Quixote, too, he stoutly affirms to be as
fitting a subject for merriment as Sancho
Panza. Both are laughable, and both are
meant to be laughed at; the extravagances of
each being pitted dexterously against those of
the other by a great artist in the ridiculous.
But he is by no means insensible to the charm
and goodness of the "ingenious gentleman;"
for sympathy is the legitimate attribute of
humor, and even where the humorist seems
most pitiless, and even brutal, in his apprehension of the absurd, he has a living tenderness
for our poor humanity which is so rich in its
absurdities.

Hazlitt's definition of wit and humor is perhaps as good as any definition is ever likely to
be; that is, it expresses a half-truth with a
great deal of reasonableness and accuracy.
"Humor," he says, "is the describing the

ludicrous as it is in itself; wit is the exposing it by comparing or contrasting it with something else. Humor is the growth of nature and accident; wit is the product of art and fancy. Humor, as it is shown in books, is an imitation of the natural or acquired absurdities of mankind, or of the ludicrous in accident, situation, and character; wit is the illustrating and heightening the sense of that absurdity by some sudden and unexpected likeness or opposition of one thing to another, which sets off the quality we laugh at or despise in a still more contemptible or striking point of view."

This is perhaps enough to show us at least one cause of the endless triumph of humor over wit, — a triumph due to its closer affinity with the simple and elementary conditions of human nature and life. Wit is artificial; humor is natural. Wit is accidental; humor is inevitable. Wit is born of conscious effort; humor, of the allotted ironies of fate. Wit can be expressed only in language; humor can be developed sufficiently in situation. Wit is the plaything of the intellectual, or the weapon of nimble minds; humor is the possession of all sorts and conditions of men. Wit is truly

what Shelley falsely imagined virtue to be,
" a refinement of civilized life ; " humor is the
property of all races in every stage of development. Wit possesses a species of immortality,
and for many generations holds its own;
humor is truly immortal, and as long as the
eye sees, and the ear hears, and the heart
beats, it will be our privilege to laugh at the
pleasant absurdities which require no other
seed or nurture than man's endless intercourse
with man.

Nevertheless, an understanding of the differ-
ences in nations and in epochs helps us to the
enjoyment of many humorous situations. We
should know something of England and of
India to appreciate the peculiar horror with
which Lord Minto, on reaching Calcutta, beheld the fourteen male attendants who stood
in his chamber, respectfully prepared to help
him into bed; or his still greater dismay at
being presented by the rajah of Bali with
seven slaves, — five little boys and two little
girls, — all of whom cost the conscientious
governor-general a deal of trouble and expense
before they were properly disposed of, and in a
fair way to learn their alphabet and catechism.

Yet perhaps a deeper knowledge of time and character is needed to sound the depths of Sir Robert Walpole's cynical observation, "Gratitude is a lively sense of future favors;" although this is indeed a type of witticism which possesses inherent vitality, not depending upon any play of words or double meanings, but striking deep root into the fundamental failings of the human heart.

It is in its simplest forms, however, that humor enjoys a world-wide actuality, and is the connecting link of all times and places and people. "Let us start from laughter," says M. Edmond Scherer, "since laughter is a thing familiar to every one. It is excited by a sense of the ridiculous, and the ridiculous arises from the contradiction between the use of a thing and its intention." Even that commonest of all themes, a fellow-creature slipping or falling, M. Scherer holds to be provocative of mirth; and in selecting this elementary example he bravely drives the matter back to its earliest and rudest principles. For it is a weapon in the hands of the serious that such casualties, which should excite instant sympathy and alarm, awaken laughter only in

those who are too foolish or too brutal to experience any other sensation. It would seem,
indeed, that the sight of a man falling on the
ice or in the mud cannot be, and ought not to
be, very amusing. But before we frown severely and forever upon such vulgar jests, let
us turn for a moment to a well-known essay,
and see what Charles Lamb has to plead in
their extenuation : —

" I am by nature extremely susceptible of
street affronts; the jeers and taunts of the
populace; the low-bred triumph they display
over the casual trip or splashed stocking of a
gentleman. Yet I can endure the jocularity
of a young sweep with something more than
forgiveness. In the last winter but one, pacing
along Cheapside with my accustomed precipi-
tation when I walk westward, a treacherous
slide brought me upon my back in an instant.
I scrambled up with pain and shame enough,
— yet outwardly trying to face it down, as if
nothing had happened, — when the roguish
grin of one of these young wits encountered
me. There he stood, pointing me out with his
dusky finger to the mob, and to a poor woman
(I suppose his mother) in particular, till the

tears for the exquisiteness of the fun (so he thought it) worked themselves out at the corners of his poor red eyes, red from many a previous weeping, and soot-inflamed, yet twinkling through all with such a joy, snatched out of desolation, that Hogarth — but Hogarth has got him already (how could he miss him?) in the March to Finchley, grinning at the pieman; — there he stood, as he stands in the picture, irremovable, as if the jest was to last forever, with such a maximum of glee and minimum of mischief in his mirth — for the grin of a genuine sweep hath absolutely no malice in it — that I could have been content, if the honor of a gentleman might endure it, to have remained his butt and his mockery till midnight."

Ah, prince of kindly humorists, to whom shall we go but to you for tears and laughter, and pastime and sympathy, and jests and gentle tolerance, and all things needed to make light our trouble-burdened hearts!

It is not worth while to deny or even to soften the cruel side of humor, though it is a far more grievous error to overlook its generous forbearance. The humorist's view of life

is essentially genial; but he has given stout
blows in his day, and the sound of his vigorous
warfare rings harshly in our unaccustomed
ears. " The old giants of English fun " were
neither soft-spoken nor soft-handed gentry,
and it seems to us now and then as if they
laid about them with joyous and indiscriminate
activity. Even Dickens, the last and greatest
of his race, and haunted often to his fall by
the beckoning of mirthless modern phantoms,
shows in his earlier work a good deal of this
gleeful and unhesitating belligerency. The
scenes between old Weller and Mr. Stiggins
might be successfully acted in a spirited
puppet-show, where conversation is of less
importance than well-timed and well-bestowed
pommeling. But we have now reached that
point of humane seriousness when even puppet-
shows cannot escape their educational respon-
sibilities, and when Punch and Judy are
gravely censured for teaching a lesson in brutality. The laughter of generations, which
should protect and hallow the little manikins
at play, counts for nothing by the side of their
irresponsible naughtiness, and their cheerful
disregard of all our moral standards. Yet

here, too, Hazlitt has a seasonable word of defense, holding indeed that he who invented such diverting pastimes was a benefactor to his species, and gave us something which it was rational and healthy to enjoy. " We place the mirth and glee and triumph to our own account," he says, " and we know that the bangs and blows the actors have received go for nothing as soon as the showman puts them up in his box, and marches off quietly with them, as jugglers of a less amusing description sometimes march off with the wrongs and rights of mankind in their pockets." It has been well said that wit requires a good head; humor, a good heart; and fun, high spirits. Punch's spirits, let us hasten to admit, are considerably in advance of his head and heart; yet nevertheless he is wanting neither in acuteness nor in the spirit of good-fellowship. He has hearkened to the advice given by Seneca many years ago, " Jest without bitterness "! and has practiced this delightful accomplishment for centuries, as befits the most conservative joker in the world.

Another reproach urged against humor rather than wit is its somewhat complicated system of lying; and much well-merited severity has been expended upon such questionable diversions as hoaxing, quizzing, "selling," and other variations of the game, the titles of which have long since passed away, leaving their substance behind them. It would be easy, but untrue, to say that real humor has nothing whatever to do with these unworthy offshoots, and never encourages their growth. The fact remains that they spring from a great humorous principle, and one which critics have been prompt to recognize, and to embody in language as clear and unmistakable as possible. "Lying," says Hazlitt, "is a species of wit and humor. To lay anything to a person's charge from which he is perfectly free shows spirit and invention; and the more incredible the effrontery the greater is the joke." "The terrors of Sancho," observes M. Scherer, "the rascalities of Scapin, the brags of Falstaff, amuse us because of their disproportion with circumstances, or their disagreement with facts." Just as Charles Lamb humanizes a brutal jest by turning it against himself, so Sir Walter Scott gives amusing emphasis to a lie by directing it against his own personality.

His description of himself in his journal as a
"pebble-hearted cur," the occasion being his
parting with the emotional Madame Mirbel, is
truly humorous, because of its remoteness from
the truth. There are plenty of men who could
have risked using the phrase without exciting
in us that sudden sense of incongruity which
is a legitimate source of laughter. A delightful instance of effrontery, which shows both
spirit and invention, is the story told by Sir
Francis Doyle of the highwayman who, having
attacked and robbed Lord Derby and his
friend Mr. Grenville, said to them with re-
proachful candor, " What scoundrels you must
be to fire at gentlemen who risk their lives
upon the road ! "   As for the wit that lies in
playful misstatements and exaggerations, we
must search for it in the riotous humor of
Lamb's letters, where the true and the false
are often so inextricably commingled that it is
a hopeless task to separate facts from fancies.
" I shall certainly go to the naughty man for
fibbing," writes Lamb, with soft laughter; and
the devout apprehension may have been justly
shared by Edward Fitzgerald, when he describes the parish church at Woodbridge as

being so damp that the fungi grew in great numbers about the communion table.

A keen sense of the absurd is so little relished by those who have it not that it is too often considered solely as a weapon of offense, and not as a shield against the countless ills that come to man through lack of sanity and judgment. There is a well-defined impression in the world that the satirist, like the devil, roams abroad, seeking whom he may devour, and generally devouring the best; whereas his position is often that of the besieged, who defends himself with the sharpest weapons at his command against a host of invading evils. There are many things in life so radically unwholesome that it is not safe to approach them save with laughter as a disinfectant; and when people cannot laugh, the moral atmosphere grows stagnant, and nothing is too morbid, too preposterous, or too mischievous to meet with sympathy and solemn assurances of good will. This is why a sense of the ridiculous has been justly called the guardian of our minor morals, rendering men in some measure dependent upon the judgments of their associates, and laying the basis of that decorum and propriety of conduct which is a necessary condition of human life, and upon which is founded the great charm of intercourse between equals. From what pitfalls of vanity and self-assurance have we been saved by this ever-watchful presence ! Into what abysmal follies have we fallen when she withholds her restraining hand ! Shelley's letters are perhaps the strongest argument in behalf of healthy humor that literature has yet offered to the world. Only a man burdened with an "invincible repugnance to the comic" could have gravely penned a sentence like this: "Certainly a saint may be amiable, — she *may* be so; but then she does not understand, — has neglected to investigate the religion which retiring, modest prejudice leads her to profess." Only a man afflicted with what Mr. Arnold mildly calls an "inhuman" lack of humor could have written thus to a female friend: "The French language you already know; and, if the great name of Rousseau did not redeem it, it would have been perhaps as well that you had remained ignorant of it." Our natural pleasure at this verdict may be agreeably heightened by placing alongside of it

Madame de Staël's moderate statement, "Conversation, like talent, exists only in France." And such robust expressions of opinion give us our clearest insight into at least one of the dangers from which a sense of the ridiculous rescues its fortunate possessor.

When all has been said, however, we must admit that edged tools are dangerous things to handle, and not infrequently do much hurt. "The art of being humorous in an agreeable way" is as difficult in our day as in the days of Marcus Aurelius, and a disagreeable exercise of this noble gift is as unwelcome now as then. "Levity has as many tricks as the kitten," says Leigh Hunt, who was quite capable of illustrating and proving the truth of his assertion, and whose scratching at times closely resembled the less playful manifestations of a full-grown cat. Wit is the salt of conversation, not the food, and few things in the world are more wearying than a sarcastic attitude towards life. "Je goûte ceux qui sont raisonnables, et me divertis des extravagants," says Uranie, in "La Critique de l'École des Femmes;" and even these words seem to tolerant ears to savor unduly of arrogance. The best use we can make

of humor is, not to divert ourselves with, but
to defend ourselves against, the folly of fools;
for much of the world's misery is entailed upon
her by her eminently well-meaning and foolish
children. There is no finer proof of Miss
Austen's matured genius than the gradual
mellowing of her humor, from the deliberate
pleasure affected by Elizabeth Bennet and her
father in the foibles of their fellow-creatures to
the amused sympathy betrayed in every page
of " Emma " and " Persuasion." Not even the
charm and brilliance of " Pride and Prejudice "
can altogether reconcile us to a heroine who,
like Uranie, diverts herself with the failings of
mankind. What a gap between Mr. Bennet's
cynical praise of his son-in-law, Wickham, —
which, under the circumstances, is a little re-
volting, — and Mr. Knightley's manly reproof
to Emma, whose youthful gayety beguiles her
into an unkind jest. While we talk much of
Miss Austen's merciless laughter, let us remember always that the finest and bravest defense
of harmless folly against insolent wit is embodied in this earnest remonstrance from the lips
of a lover who is courageous enough to speak
plain truths, with no suspicion of priggishness
to mar their wholesome flavor.

It is difficult, at any time, to deprive wit of its social or political surroundings ; it is impossible to drive it back to those deeper, simpler sources whence humor springs unveiled. " Hudibras," for example, is witty ; " Don Quixote " is humorous. Sheridan is witty ; Goldsmith is humorous. To turn from the sparkling scenes where the Rivals play their mimic parts to the quiet fireside where the Vicar and Farmer Flamborough sit sipping their gooseberry wine is to reënter life, and to feel human hearts beating against our own. How delicate the touch which puts everything before us with a certain gentle, loving malice, winning us to laughter, without for a moment alienating our sympathies from the right. Hazlitt claims for the wicked and witty comedies of the Restoration that it is their privilege to allay our scruples and banish our just regrets ; but when Goldsmith brings the profligate squire and his female associates into the Vicar's innocent household, the scene is one of pure and incomparable humor, which nevertheless leaves us more than ever in love with the simple goodness which is so readily deceived. Mr. Thornhill utters a questionable sentiment. The two fine ladies, who have been striving hard to play their parts, and only letting slip occasional oaths, affect great displeasure at his laxness, and at once begin a very discreet and serious dialogue upon virtue. " In this my wife, the chaplain, and I soon joined ; and the squire himself was at last brought to confess a sense of sorrow for his former excesses. We talked of the pleasures of temperance, and of the sunshine of the mind unpolluted with guilt. I was so well pleased that my little ones were kept up beyond the usual time, to be edified by so much good conversation. Mr. Thornhill even went beyond me, and demanded if I had any objection to giving prayers. I joyfully embraced the proposal ; and in this manner the night was passed in a most comfortable way, till at length the company began to think of returning." What a picture it is ! What an admirably humorous situation ! What easy tolerance in the treatment ! We laugh, but even in our laughter we know that not for the space of a passing breath does Goldsmith yield his own sympathy, or divert ours, away from the just cause of innocence and truth.

If men of real wit have been more numerous in the world than men of real humor, it is
because discernment and lenity, mirth and
conciliation, are qualities which do not blend
easily with the natural asperity of our race.
Humor has been somewhat daringly defined as
" a sympathy for the seamy side of things."
It does not hover on the borders of the light
and trifling; it does not linger in that keen
and courtly atmosphere which is the chosen
playground of wit; but diffusing itself subtly
throughout all nature, reveals to us life, — life
which we love to consider and to judge from
some pet standpoint of our own, but which is so
big and wonderful, and good and bad, and fine
and terrible, that our little peaks of observation command only a glimpse of the mysteries
we are so ready and willing to solve. Thus, the
degree of wit embodied in an old story is a matter of much dispute and of scant importance;
but when we read that Queen Elizabeth, in her
last illness, turned wearily away from matters
of state, " yet delighted to hear some of the
' Hundred Merry Tales,' and to such was very
attentive," we feel we have been lifted into
the regions of humor, and by its sudden light

we recognize, not the dubious merriment of the
tales, but the sick and world-worn spirit seeking a transient relief from fretful care and
poisonous recollections. So, too, when Sheridan said of Mr. Dundas that he resorted to
his memory for his jests, and to his imagination for his facts, the great wit, after the
fashion of wits, expressed a limited truth. It
was a delightful statement so far as it went,
but it went no further than Mr. Dundas, with
just the possibility of a second application.
When Voltaire sighed, "Nothing is so disagreeable as to be obscurely hanged," he gave
utterance to a national sentiment, which is not
in the least witty, but profoundly humorous,
revealing with charming distinctness a Frenchman's innate aversion to all dull and commonplace surroundings. Dying is not with him,
as with an Englishman, a strictly " private af-
fair ; " it is the last act of life's brilliant play,
which is expected to throw no discredit upon
the sparkling scenes it closes.

The breadth of atmosphere which humor
requires for its development, the saneness and
sympathy of its revelations, are admirably
described by one of the most penetrating and

least humorous of French critics, M. Edmond
Scherer, whose words are all the more grateful
and valuable to us when they refer, not to his
own countrymen, but to those robust English
humorists whom it is our present pleasure to
ignore. M. Scherer, it is true, finds much
fault, and reasonable fault ever, with these
stout-hearted, strong-handed veterans. They
are not always decorous. They are not always
sincere. They are wont to play with their
subjects. They are too eager to amuse themselves and other people. It is easy to make
out a list of their derelictions. " Yet this does
not prevent the temperament of the humorist
from being, on the whole, the happiest that a
man can bring with him into this world, nor
his point of view from being the fairest from
which the world can be judged. The satirist
grows wroth; the cynic banters; the humorist
laughs and sympathizes by turns. . . . He has
neither the fault of the pessimist, who refers
everything to a purely personal conception,
and is angry with reality for not being such
as he conceives it; nor that of the optimist,
who shuts his eyes to everything missing on
the real earth, that he may comply with the

demands of his heart and of his reason. The humorist feels the imperfections of reality, and resigns himself to them with good temper, knowing that his own satisfaction is not the rule of things, and that the formula of the universe is necessarily larger than the preferences of a single one of the accidental beings of whom the universe is composed. He is beyond doubt the true philosopher."

This is a broad statement; yet to endure life smilingly is no ignoble task; and if the humors of mankind are inseparably blended with all their impulses and actions, it is worth while to consider bravely the value of qualities so subtle and far-reaching in their influences. Steele, as we know, dressed the invading bailiffs in liveries, and amazed his guests by the number and elegance of his retainers. Sydney Smith fastened antlers on his sheep, for the gratification of a lady who thought he ought to have deer in his park. Such elaborate jests, born of invincible gayety and high spirits, seem childish to our present adult seriousness; and we are too impatient to understand that they represent an attitude, and a very healthy attitude, towards life. The

iniquity of Steele's career lay in his repeatedly
running into debt, not in the admirable temper
with which he met the consequences of that
debt when they were forced upon him; and
if the censorious are disposed to believe that
a less happy disposition would have avoided
these consequences, let them consider the ca-
reers of poor Richard Savage and other mis-
anthropic prodigals. As for Sydney Smith,
he followed Burton's excellent counsel, " Go
on then merrily to heaven ; " and his path was
none the less straight because it was smoothed
by laughter. That which must be borne had
best be borne cheerfully, and sometimes a
single telling stroke of wit, a single word rich
in manly humor, reveals to us that true courage, that fine philosophy, which endures and
even tolerates the vicissitudes of fortune,
without for a moment relinquishing its honest
hold upon the right. Mr. Lang has told us
such a little story of the verger in a Saxon
town who was wont to show visitors a silver
mouse, which had been offered by the women
to the Blessed Virgin that she might rid the
town of mice. A Prussian officer, with that
prompt brutality which loves to offend religious

sentiment it does not share, asked jeeringly,
" Are you such fools as to believe that the
creatures went away because a silver mouse
was dedicated ? "   " Ah, no," replied the verger, " or long ago we should have offered a
silver Prussian."

It is the often-expressed opinion of Leigh
Hunt that although wit and humor may be
found in perfection apart from each other, yet
their best work is shared in common. Wit
separated from humor is but an element of
sport; "a laughing jade," with petulant
whims and fancies, which runs away with our
discretion, confuses our wisdom, and mocks at
holy charity; yet adds greatly, withal, to the
buoyancy and popularity of life. It makes
gentlefolk laugh, — a difficult task, says Mo-
lière ; it scatters our faculties, and " bears
them off deridingly into pastime." It is a
fire-gleam in our dull world, a gift of the gods,
who love to provide weapons for the amusement and discomfiture of mankind. But humor stands on common soil, and breathes our
common air. The kindly contagion of its
mirth lifts our hearts from their personal apprehension of life's grievances, and links us

together in a bond of mutual tears and laughter. If it be powerless to mould existence, or even explain it to our satisfaction, it can give us at least some basis for philosophy, some scope for sympathy, and sanity, and endurance. " The perceptions of the contrasts of human destiny," says M. Scherer, " by a man who does not sever himself from humanity, but who takes his own shortcomings and those of his dear fellow-creatures cheerfully, — this is the essence of humor."

LETTERS.

IT is one of the current complaints of to-day that the art of letter-writing, as our great-grandfathers and our great-great-grandfathers knew it, has been utterly and irrevocably lost. Railways, which bring together easily and often people who used to spend the greater portion of their lives apart; cheap postage, which relieves a man from any serious responsibility for what he writes, — the most insignificant scrawl seems worth the stamp he puts on it; the hurried, restless pace at which we live, each day filled to the brim with things which are hardly so important as we think them, and which have cost us the old rich hours of leisurely thought and inaction, — these are the forces which have conspired to destroy the letter, and to crowd into its place that usurping and unprofitable little upstart called the note. "The art of note-writing," says Mr. Bagehot, "may become classical; it is for the present age to provide models for that sort of composition; but letters have perished. In the last century, cultivated people who sat down to write took pains to have something to say, and took pains to say it. The correspondence of to-day is like a series of telegrams with amplified headings. There is not more than one idea, and that idea soon comes and is soon over. The best correspondence of the past is rather like a good light article, in which the points are studiously made; in which the effort to make them is studiously concealed; in which a series of selected circumstances is set forth; in which you feel, but are not told, that the principle of the writer's selection was to make his composition pleasant."

It is difficult not to agree with Mr. Bagehot and other critics who have uttered similar lamentations. The letter which resembled a good light article has indeed disappeared from our midst, and I am not sure that many dry eyes have not witnessed its departure. Light articles are now provided for us in such generous measure by our magazines that we have scant need to exact them from our friends. In fact, we should have no time to read them, if they were written. A more serious loss is the total absence of any minute information or gossip upon current topics in the mass of modern correspondence. The letter which is so useful to historians, which shows us, and shows us as nothing else can ever do, the ordinary, every-day life of prominent men and women, this letter has also disappeared, and there is nothing to take its place. We can reconstruct the England, or at least the London of George II. and George III. from the pages of Horace Walpole. Who is there likely to hand down in this fashion to a coming generation the England of Queen Victoria? Neither does the fact of Walpole's being by no means a bigot in the matter of truth-telling interfere with his real value. He lies consciously and with a set purpose here and there; he is unconsciously and even inevitably veracious in the main. There are some points, observes Mr. Bagehot, on which almost everybody's letters are true. " The delineation of a recurring and familiar life is beyond the reach of a fraudulent fancy. Horace Walpole was not a very scrupulous narrator, yet it was too much trouble, even for him, to tell lies

on many things. His stories and conspicuous scandals are no doubt often unfounded;
but there is a gentle undercurrent of daily
unremarkable life and manners which he
evidently assumed as a datum for his histor-
ical imagination."

We may be quite sure, for example, on his
testimony, that people of fashion went to
Ranelagh two hours after the music was over,
because it was thought vulgar to go earlier;
that Lord Derby's cook gave him warning,
rather than dress suppers at three o'clock in
the morning; that when a masked ball was
given by eighteen young noblemen at Soho,
the mob in the street stopped the fine coaches,
held up torches to the windows, and demanded
to have the masks pulled off and put on at
their pleasure, "but all with extreme good-
humor and civility;" that he, Horace Walpole, one night at Vauxhall, helped Lady
Caroline Petersham to mince seven chickens
in a china dish, which chickens "Lady Caroline stewed over a lamp, with three pats of
butter and a flagon of water, stirring and rat-
tling and laughing, and we every minute ex-
pecting to have the dish fly about our ears;"

that at the funeral of George II., the Duke of
Newcastle — that curious burlesque of an English nobleman — stood on the train of the
butcher Duke of Cumberland to avoid the chill
of the marble. If we think these things are
not worth knowing, we had better not read
Walpole's letters, for these are the things
which he delights in telling us. Macaulay
thought these things were not worth knowing,
and he has accordingly branded Walpole as a
superficial observer, a vain and shallow world-
ling. How, he wonders, can we listen seriously
to a man who haunted auctions; who collected
bricabrac; who sat up all night playing cards
with fine, frivolous ladies; who liked being
a fashionable gentleman, and had no proper
pride in belonging to the august assemblage
of authors; and who, most deadly crime of all,
lived face to face with the great Whig leaders
of the day, and was not in the least impressed
by the magnitude of the distinction thus con-
ferred on him. But, after all, we cannot, every
one of us, be built upon the same solemn and
righteous lines. It is not even granted to
every one to be a fervent and consistent Whig.
Horace Walpole, you see, was Horace Wal-

pole, and not Thomas Babington Macaulay: therefore Macaulay despised him, and called on all his readers to despise him too. We can only have recourse to Mr. Lang's philosophy : " 'T is a wide world, my masters; there is room for both." Walpole is the prince of letter-writers, because writing letters was the inspiration, the ruling passion of his life, and he was preëminently qualified for the task. It has been well said that had some evil chance wrecked him, like Robinson Crusoe, upon a desert island, he would have gone on writing letters just the same, and waited for a ship to carry them away. This is a pleasant conceit, because the spectacle of Horace Walpole on a desert island is one which captivates the idle fancy. Think of his little airs and graces, his courtly affectations, his fine clothes and frippery, his dainty epicureanism, his sense of good comradeship, all thrown away upon a desert island, and upon the society of a parrot and a goat. What malicious tales he would have been forced to invent about the parrot! It is best not to believe evil of any one upon Walpole's word, especially not of any one who had ever attacked Sir Robert's ministry; for

Horace's filial piety took the very exclusive
form of undying enmity to all his father's political opponents. But when we have passed
over and tried to forget all that is spiteful and
caustic and coarse in these celebrated letters,
there is a great deal left, a great deal that is
not even the current gossip of the day. He
goes to Paris in 1765, and finds that laughing
is out of fashion in that once gay capital.
"Good folks!" he cries, "they have no time
to laugh. There are God and the king to be
pulled down first, and men and women, one
and all, are devoutly employed in the demoli-
tion. They think me quite profane for having
my belief left." A few years later, Walpole
sees clearly that French politics must end in
"despotism, a civil war, or assassination."
The age is not, he says, as he once thought,
an age of abortion; but rather "an age of
seeds which are to produce strange crops here-
after." Surely, even Macaulay might allow
that these are the words of a thinker, of a
prophet, perhaps, standing unheeded in the
market-place.

Granted, then, that the light-article letter,
and the letter which gives us material with

which to fill up the gaps and crannies of history, which holds the life of the past embalmed in its faded pages, have disappeared, perhaps forever. There is another letter which has not disappeared, which never can disappear as long as man stays man and woman, woman, — the letter which reveals to us the personality of the writer; which is dear and valuable to us because in it his hand stretches out frankly from the past, and draws us to his side. It may be long or short, carefully or carelessly written, full of useful information or full of idle nonsense. We do not stop to ask. It is enough for us to know from whom it came. And the finest type of such a letter may surely be found in the well-loved correspondence of Charles Lamb. If we eliminated from his pages all critical matter, all those shrewd and admirable verdicts upon prose and verse; if we cut out ruthlessly such scraps of news as they occasionally convey; if we banished all references to celebrated people, from the "obnoxious squeak" of Shelley's voice to the generous sympathy expressed for Napoleon, we should still have left — the writer himself, which is all that we desire. We should still

have the record of that harmless and patient,
that brave and sorely tried life. We should
still see infinite mirth and infinite pathos interwoven upon every page. We should catch the
echo of that clear, kind laughter which never
hardens into scorn. Lamb laughs at so many
people, and never once wrongs any one. We
should see the flashes of a wit which carries no
venom in its sting. We should feel that atmosphere of wonderful, whimsical humor illumi-
nating all the trivial details of existence. We
should recognize in the turning of every sentence, the conscious choice of every word, the
fine and distinctive qualities of a genius that
has no parallel.

It matters little at what page we read. Here
is the sad story of Henry Robinson's waistcoat,
which Mary Lamb tried to bring over from
France, but which was seized at the Custom
House, " for the use of the king," says
Charles dryly. " He will probably appear in it
at the next levee." Here is the never-to-be-
forgotten tea-party at Miss Benjay's, where
that tenth-rate little upstart of a woman —
type of a genus that survives to-day — alter.
nately patronized and snubbed her guest;

flinging at him her pitiful scraps of information, marveling that he did not understand French, insulting him when he ventured an opinion upon poetry, — " seeing that it was my own trade in a manner," — imparting to him Hannah More's valuable dogmas on education, feeding him scantily with macaroons, and sending him home, — not angry as he had a right to be, as any other man would have been in his place, only infinitely amused. And then some people say that a keen sense of the ridiculous is not a kindly sentiment! It is, we know it is, when we read the letter to Coleridge in which Lamb tells how he went to condole with poor Joseph Cottle on the death of his brother Amos, and how, as the readiest comfort he could offer, he swiftly introduced into his conversation Joseph's epic poem, " Alfred," luring the mourner gently from his grief by arousing his poetic vanity. The dear, good, stupid Cottle, brightening visibly under such soothing treatment, fixed upon his visitor a benevolent gaze, and prepared himself for melancholy enjoyment. After a while the name of Alswitha, Alfred's queen, was slipped adroitly into the discourse. " At that mo-

ment," says Lamb, "I could perceive that
Cottle had forgot his brother was so lately become a blessed spirit. In the language of
mathematicians, the author was as nine, the
brother as one. I felt my cue, and strong pity
stirring at the root, I went to work." So the
little comedy proceeds, until it reaches its cli-
max when George Dyer, to whom all poems
were good poems, remarks that the dead Amos
was estimable both for his head and heart, and
would have made a fine poet if he had lived.
"To this," says Lamb, "Joseph fully assented,
but could not help adding that he always
thought the qualities of his brother's heart ex-
ceeded those of his head. I believe his brother,
when living, had formed precisely the same
idea of him; and I apprehend the world will
assent to both judgments." Now if we will but
try to picture to ourselves how Carlyle would
have behaved to poor Miss Benjay, how Walpole would have sneered at Joseph Cottle, we
will understand better the harmless, the almost loving nature of Charles Lamb's raillery,
which we can enjoy so frankly because it gave
no pain.

As for the well-known fact that Lamb's let-

ters reflect nothing of the political tumult, the
stirring warfare, amid which he lived, it is
interesting to place by their side the contem-
porary letters of Sir Gilbert Elliot, the first
Earl of Minto, a correspondence the princi-
pal charm of which is the revelation it makes
of a nature so fine and brave, so upright and
honorable, so wise and strong and good, that
we can best understand the secret of England's
greatness when we know she has given birth
to such sons. To study the life of a man who
played so prominent a part in home and foreign
politics is to study the history of Europe during those troubled years. In Lord Minto's
letters we follow breathlessly the desperate
struggle with Napoleon, the ceaseless wran-
gling of the Allies, the dangerous rebellions in
Ireland, the grave perplexities of the Indian
empire ; and besides these all-important topics,
we have side-lights thrown upon social life.
We learn, for instance, that Mrs. Crewe, the
celebrated beauty and toast of the Whigs,
liked good conversation, and took an interest
and even a part, writes Sir Gilbert naïvely to
his wife, " in all subjects which men would
naturally talk of when *not* in woman's com-

pany, as politics and literature." We learn
also — what we half suspected before — that
Madame de Staël was so greedy of admiration that she was capable of purchasing "any
quantity of anybody at any price, and among
other prices by a traffic of mutual flattery;"
and that she was never satisfied unless she
could have the whole conversation to herself,
and be the centre of every company.

Now, it is hardly to be expected that the
letters of a great statesman and the letters of
an obscure clerk in the India House should
reveal precisely the same interests and information, any more than it is to be expected that
the letters of the statesman — who was, after
all, a statesman and no more — should equal
in literary charm and merit the letters of the
clerk who was in addition an immortal genius.
But when we think how profoundly England
was shaken and disturbed by the discords and
apprehensions of those troubled times, how
wars and the rumors of wars darkened the
air, and stirred the blood of country bump-
kins and placid rural squires, it seems a little
strange that Lamb, who lived long years in
the heart of London, and must have heard

so much of these things, should have written about them so little. He does learn when there is a change of ministry, because he hears a butcher say something about it in the market-place. He cultivates a frank admiration for Napoleon, whom all his countrymen hated and feared so madly. He would be glad, he says, to stand bareheaded at his table, doing honor to him in his fall. And, after the battle of Trafalgar, he writes to Hazlitt: "Lord Nelson is quiet at last. His ghost only keeps a slight fluttering in odes and elegies in newspapers, and impromptus which could not be got ready before the funeral."

These characteristic passages and others like them are all we hear of public matters from Charles Lamb, and few of us would ask for more. It is the continual sounding of the personal note that makes his pages so dear to us; it is the peculiarly restful character of his beloved chit-chat that keeps them so fresh and delightful. And while there is but one Lamb, there are many letters which have in them something of this same personal quality, something of this restful charm. The supply can never be exhausted, because letter-writing —

not light articles now, nor brilliant semi-historic narratives, but real letter-writing — is founded on a need as old and as young as humanity itself, the need that one human being has of another. The craving for sympathy; the natural and healthy egotism which prompts us to open our minds to absent friends; the desire we all feel to make known to others that which is happening to ourselves; the certainty we all feel that others will be profoundly interested in this revelation; the inextinguishable impulse to "pass on" experiences either of soul or body, to share with some one else that which we are hearing, or seeing, or feeling, or suffering, or enjoying, — these are the motives which make letter-writing essential and inevitable, crowd it into the busiest lives, assimilate it with the dullest understandings, and fit it into some crevice of every one's daily experience. Thus it happens that there is a strong family resemblance between letters of every age and every country; they really change less than we are pleased to think. The Rev. Augustus Jessopp, in one of his delightful essays, quotes from a long and chatty letter written, about the time that

Moses was a little lad, by an Egyptian gentleman named Pambesa to a friend named Amenemapt, and giving a very lively and minute
account of the city of Rameses, which Pambesa was then happily visiting for the first
time. We have all of us had just such letters from our absent friends, and have read
them with mingled pleasure, and envy, and irritation. Pambesa the traveler is not disposed
to spare Amenemapt the stay-at-home any detail of what he is missing. Never was there
such a city of the gods as this particular town
of Rameses which Amenemapt was not destined to see. There might be found the best
of good living ; vines, and fig-trees, and onion
beds, and nursery gardens. Stout drinkers
too were its jovial inhabitants, with a variety
of strong liquors, sweet syrups richer than
honey, red wine, and very excellent imported
beer. Its women were all well dressed, and
curled their hair enticingly, smoothing it with
sweet oil. They stood at their doors, holding nosegays in their hands, and presenting
a very alluring appearance to this gay and
shameless Pambesa, who could hardly make up
his mind to pass them coldly by. Altogether,

Rameses was an exceedingly pleasant town to visit, and the Egyptian gentleman was having a very jolly time of it, and we, reading his correspondence, fall to thinking that human nature before the Exodus was uncommonly like human nature to-day. This is one of the delights of letter-reading, that it reveals to us, not only the life of the past, but, better still, the people of the past, our brothers and sisters who, being dead, still live in their written pages. For the scholar the interest lies in what Pambesa has to tell; for the rest of us the interest lies in Pambesa himself, who, so many thousand years ago, drank the bitter beer, and stared at the pretty girls standing curled and flower-bedecked, with those demure, faint smiles which centuries cannot alter or impair.

So it continues, as we run swiftly down the years, the bulk of correspondence increasing enormously at every stage, until we reach such monuments of industry as the famous Cecil letters, preserved at Hatfield, and comprising over thirty thousand documents. It is pleasant to feel we need read none of these, and that, if we search for character, we may find it in thirty words as well as in thirty thousand rolls of musty parchment. We may find it surely in that historic note dispatched by Ann, Countess of Dorset, to Sir Joseph Williamson, Secretary of State under Charles II., who wanted her to appoint a courtier as member from Appleby. Nothing could well be shorter; nothing could possibly be more significant. This is all : —

SIR, — I have been bullied by an usurper, I have been ill-treated by a court, but I won't be dictated to by a subject. Your man shall not stand.

ANN DORSET, PEMBROKE AND MONTGOMERY.

Now if you don't feel you know Ann Dorset pretty well after reading those four lines, you would n't know her if she left a diary as long as Samuel Pepys's ; and if you don't feel, after reading them, that she is worth the knowing, it is hopeless for her to try and win your regard. Another and still more amusing instance of self-revelation may be found in a manuscript familiar to many who have visited the Bodleian Library at Oxford. There, among other precious treasures, is a collection of notes scribbled by Charles II. to Clarendon, and by Clarendon to Charles II., to beguile the tedium of Council. They look, for all the world, like the notes which school-girls are wont to scribble to one another, to beguile the tedium of study. On one page, Charles in a little careless hand, not unlike a school-girl's, writes that he wants to go to Tunbridge, to see his sister. Clarendon in larger, firmer characters writes back that there is no reason why he should not, if he can return in a few days, and adds tentatively, " I suppose you will go with a light train." Charles, as though glowing with conscious rectitude, responds, " I intend to take nothing but my night-bag." Clarendon, who knows his master's luxurious habits, is startled out of all propriety. " Gods! " he writes : " you will not go without forty or fifty horse." Then Charles, who seems to have been waiting for this point in the dialogue, tranquilly replies in one straggling line at the bottom of the page. " I count that part of my night-bag." How plainly we can hear the royal chuckle which accompanied this gracious explanation! How really valuable is this scrap of correspondence which shows us for a moment Charles Stuart; not the Charles

of Sir Walter's loyal stories, nor the Charles
of Macaulay's eloquent invectives; but Charles
himself, our fellow mortal, and a very human
character indeed.

If, as Mr. Bagehot affirms, it is for the present day to provide models which shall make
the art of note-writing classical, we can begin
no better than by studying the specimens already in our keeping. If we want humor,·
pathos, a whole tale told in half a dozen words,
we have these things already in every sentence
of Steele's hasty scrawls to his wife : " Prue,
Prue, look a little dressed, and be beautiful."
— And again : " 'T is the glory of a Woman,
Prue, to be her husband's Friend and Companion, and not his Sovereign Director." — Or
" Good-nature, added to that beautiful form
God has given you, would make an happinesse
too great for Humane life." — And finally,
" I am, dear Prue, a little in Drink, but at
all times, Your Faithful Husband, Richard
Steele."

These bare scraps of letters, briefer, many
of them, than the " scandalous half-sheets "
which Prue was wont to send in return, give
us a tolerably clear insight into the precise

nature of Steele's domestic happiness. We understand, not only the writer, but the recipient of such missives, poor petulant Prue, who has had scant mercy shown her in Thackeray's brilliant pages, but whose own life was not passed upon a bed of roses. We are eager to catch these swift glimpses of real people through a few careless lines which have miraculously escaped destruction; or perhaps through a brief aside in an important, but, to us, very uninteresting communication; as, for example, when Marlborough reopens a dispatch to say that he has just received word of the surprise and defeat of the Dutch general, Opdam. "Since I sealed my letter," he writes with characteristic dryness, "we have a report from Breda that Opdam is beaten. I pray God it be not so, for he is very capable of having it happen to him." It is difficult not to enjoy this, because, if we sat within the shadow of Marlborough's tent, we could not hear him more distinctly; and the desire we feel to get nearer to the people who interest us, to know them as they really were, is, in the main, natural and wholesome. Yet there must be some limit set to the gratification of this desire, if

we are to check the unwarranted publishing
of private letters which has become the recognized disgrace of literature. It is hard for us
to understand just when our curiosity ceases to
be permissible; it is harder still for editors to
understand just when their privileges cease to
be beneficial. Not many years ago it was possible for Mr. Bagehot to say that he took comfort in thinking of Shelley as a poet about
whom our information was mercifully incomplete. Thanks to Professor Dowden, it is incomplete no longer; but we have scant cause
to congratulate ourselves on what we have
gained by his disclosures. Mr. Froude, acting
up to an heroic theory of friendship, has pil-
loried Carlyle for the pleasure and the pain of
gaping generations; but there are some who
turn away with averted eyes from the sordid,
shameful spectacle. Within the last decade
the reading world welcomed with acclamations
a volume of letters from the pen of one who
had made it his especial request that no
such correspondence should ever be published.
How many of those who laughed over the
witty, whimsical, intimate, affectionate outpourings of Thackeray paused to consider

that they would one and all have remained un-
written, could their author have foreseen their
fate. They were not meant for us, they never
would have reached us, had his known desires
and prejudices been respected. Many of them
are delightful, as when he tells with sedate
humor of his absurd proposal to Macaulay
that they should change identities at Sir
George Napier's dinner, so as to confuse and
baffle a young American woman, the desire of
whose heart was to meet these two great lions,
and of Macaulay's disgust at the bare notion
of jesting with anything so serious as his literary reputation. Yet when the recipient of
these letters yielded to the temptation of publishing them, she would have done well to sup-
press those trivial, colorless, and private communications which can have no possible value
or interest to others. An invitation to dinner
is of some importance the day that it arrives,
but it loses its vitality when reprinted forty
years after the dinner is eaten. There is horror in the thought that a man of genius can
never promise himself that grateful privacy
which is the lot of his happier and less distinguished brothers; but that after he has died in

the least ostentatious manner he knows how, the whole wide world is made acquainted with his diversions and his digestion, with his feeblest jokes and his most tender confidences. The problem of what to give and what to withhold must be solved by editors who, having laboriously collected their material, feel a natural disposition to use it. When, as occasionally happens, the editor regards the author simply as his prey, he never conceives the desirability of withholding anything. He is as unreserved as a savage, and probably defends himself, as did Montaigne when reproached for the impropriety of his essays, by saying that if people do not like details of that description they certainly take great pains to read them.

Among the letters too charming to be lost, yet too personal and frankly confiding to be read without some twinges of conscience, are those of Edward Fitzgerald, the last man in all England to have coveted such posthumous publicity. They reveal truthfully that kind, shy, proud, indolent, indifferent, and intensely conservative nature ; a scholar without the prick of ambition, a critic with no desire to be judicial, an unwearied mind turned aside from healthy and normal currents of activity. Yet the indiscreet publishing of a private opinion, a harmless bit of criticism such as any man has a right to express to a friend, drew down upon this least aggressive of authors abuse too coarse to be quoted. It is easy to say that Browning dishonored himself rather than Fitzgerald by the brutality of his language. This is true; but, nevertheless, it is not pleasant to go down to posterity branded with Billingsgate by a great poet; and it is doubly hard to bear such a weight of vituperation because a word said in a letter has been ruthlessly given to the world.

The unhesitating fashion in which women reveal themselves to their correspondents makes it seem treachery to read their printed pages. Those girlish confidences of Jane Austen to Cassandra, so frank and gay, so full of jokes and laughter, and country gossip, and sisterly affection, what a contrast they afford to the attitude of unbroken reserve which Miss Austen always presented to the world! Yet now the world is free to follow each foolish little jest, and to pass judgment on the wit it

holds. Those affectionate and not over-wise
outpourings of Miss Mitford, with their effusive
terms of endearment; those dignified and solemn reflections of Sara Coleridge, humanized
occasionally by a chance remark about the
baby, or an inadvertent admission that she has
gone down twice to supper at an evening party;
those keen, combative, brilliant letters of Mrs.
Carlyle that are so bitter-sweet; those unreserved and purely personal communications of
Geraldine Jewsbury which have no message
whatever for the public; — how much has been
given us to which we show scant claim! It is
true that in the days when the Polite Letter-
Writer ruled the land, and his baleful influence
was felt on every side, a great many women
wrote elaborate missives which nobody now
wants to read, but which were then more highly
prized than the gossiping pages we have learned
to love so well. These sedate blue-stockings
told neither their own affairs nor their neighbors'; but confined themselves to dignified gen-
eralities, expressed with Johnsonian elegance.
There was Miss Seward, for example, who at
times was too ridiculous for even Scott's genial
forbearance; yet whose letters won her such a

reputation that we find them diligently sought for, years after they were penned. Fancy admiring groups of men and women listening to Miss Seward's celebrated epistles to Miss Rogers and Miss Weston, one of which begins : —

" Soothing and welcome to me, dear Sophia, is the regret you express for our separation! Pleasant were the weeks we have recently passed together in this ancient and embowered mansion. I had strongly felt the silence and vacancy of the depriving day on which you vanished. How prone are our hearts perversely to quarrel with the friendly coercion of employment, at the very instant in which it is clearing the torpid and injurious mists of unavailing melancholy."

The letter which opens in this promising manner closes, as might be expected, with a fervent and glowing apostrophe to the absent one : —

" Virtuous friendship, how pure, how sacred are thy delights ! Sophia, thy mind is capable of tasting them in all their poignancy. Against how many of life's incidents may that capacity be considered as a counterpoise."

Now, in the last century, when people received letters of this kind, they did not, as we might suppose, laugh and tear them up. They treasured them sacredly in their desks, and read them to their young nieces and nephews, and made fair copies of them for less favored friends. Yet the same mail-bags which groaned under these ponderous compositions were laden now and then with Sir Walter's delightful pages, all aglow with that diffused spirit of healthy enjoyment, that sane and happy knowledge of life, that dauntless and incomparable courage. Perhaps they carried some of Cowper's letters, rich mines of pleasure and profit for us all, full to the brim of homely pleasant details which only leisure can find time to note. A man who was even ordinarily busy would never have stopped to observe the things which Cowper tells us about so charmingly, — the bustling candidate kissing all the maids ; the hungry beggar who declines to eat vermicelli soup ; the young thief who is whipped for stealing the butcher's iron-work ; the kitchen table which is scrubbed into paralysis; the retinue of kittens in the barn ; the foolish old cat who must needs pursue a viper crawling in the sun ;

and the favorite tabby who ungratefully ran
away into a ditch, and cost the family four
shillings before she was recovered. Cowper
had time to see all these things, had time to
hear the soft click of Mrs. Unwin's knitting-
needles, and the hum of the boiling tea-kettle;
and he had moreover the faculty of bringing
all that he saw and heard very vividly before
our eyes, of interesting us, almost against our
will, in the petty annals of an uneventful life.
It is no more possible for important city men,
heads of banking-houses and hard-working
members of Parliament, to write letters of this
kind, than it is possible for them to hold the
attention of generations, as Gray so easily
holds it, with a few playful lines of condolence
on the death of a friend's cat, a few polished
verses set like jewels in the delicate filigree of
a sportive and caressing letter. "It would be
a sensible satisfaction to me," he writes to
Walpole, "before I testify my sorrow, and the
sincere part I take in your misfortune, to know
for certain who it is I lament. I knew Zara
and Selima (Selima, was it? or Fatima?), or
rather I knew them both together; for I cannot justly say which was which. Then as to

your 'handsome Cat,' the name you distinguish
her by, I am no less at a loss, as well knowing
one's handsome cat is always the cat one loves
best; or if one be alive and one dead, it is
usually the latter which is the handsomer.
Besides, if the point were never so clear, I
hope you do not think me so ill-bred or so
imprudent as to forfeit all my interest in the
survivor. Oh, no! I would rather seem to
mistake, and imagine to be sure it must be
the tabby one that has met with this sad
accident."

Labor accomplishes many things in this
busy, tired world, and receives her full share
of applause for every nail she drives. But
leisure writes the letters; leisure aided by
observation, and sometimes — as in the case
of Mme. de Sévigné — by that rare faculty of
receiving and imparting impressions without
judicial reasoning, by that winning, unconten-
tious amenity which accepts life as it is, and
men as they chance to be. There is no rancor
in the light laugh with which this charming
Frenchwoman greets the follies and frivolities
of her day. There is no moral protest in
her amused survey of that attractive invalid,

Mme. de Brissac, who lies in bed so "curled and beautiful" that she turns everybody's head. "I wish you could have seen," writes Mme. de Sévigné to her daughter, "the use she made of her sufferings; of her eyes, of her sighs, of her arms, of her hands languishing on the counterpane, of the situation, and the compassion she excited. I was overcome with tenderness and admiration as I gazed on the performance, which seemed to me so fine. My riveted attention must surely have given satisfaction; and bear in mind that it was for the Abbé Bayard, for Saint Herens, for Montjeu and Plancy, that the scene was rehearsed. When I remember with what simplicity *you* are ill, you seem to me a mere bungler in comparison."

This is good-natured ridicule, keen but not condemnatory, without mercy, yet without upbraiding. Sainte-Beuve, who dearly loves Mme. de Sévigné, complains with reason that she is not even angry at things which ought to anger her, and that this gentle tolerance lacks humanity when cruelty and wrong-doing call for denunciation. Yet who can remember so long and tenderly a friend fallen and disgraced? Who can extend a helping hand so frankly to a fellow mortal? Who can love so devotedly, or sacrifice herself with such cheerful serenity at the shrine of her deep affections? Her memory comes down to us through two centuries, enriched with graceful fancies. We know her as one good and gay, gentle and witty and wise, who, by virtue of her supreme and narrowed genius, wrote letters unsurpassed in literature. "Keep my correspondence," said Lady Mary Wortley Montagu in the heyday of her youth and pride. "It will be as good as Mme. de Sévigné's, forty years hence." But four times forty years have only served to widen the gulf between these two writers, and to place them in parted spheres. Their work springs from different sources, and is as unlike in inspiration as in form. "It is impossible," says Sainte-Beuve, "to speak of women without first putting one's self in a good humor by the thought of Mme. de Sévigné. With us moderns, this process takes the place of one of those invocations or libations which the ancients were used to offer up to the pure source of grace." In the same devout spirit I am glad to close my volume with a few words about this incomparable letter-writer, with a little libation poured at her shadowy feet, that my last page may leave me and — Heaven permitting — my readers in a good humor, cheered by the pleasant memories which gild a passing hour.